On the cover is the photo of C
favorite wife on horseback in
(fro

#1. "Sacajawea"

The statue of Sacajawea stands at the entrance to the Boise Historical Museum in Boise, Idaho. Sacajawea, a Lemhi Shoshoni Indian was taken captive by the Hidatsa Indians, as a teenager. Charbonneau won Sacajawea in a gambling game and took her as his third wife, in Indian tradition. (Author Photo)

#2. "Pueblo Woman"
Courtesy Azusa Publishing Company, LLC

The Horse Indians

Robert D. Bolen, B.A.

Dedication Page

I dedicate this work
to my beautiful wife, Doris Anne

#3. "Newspaper Rock"
Indian Petroglyphs on Rock
Courtesy Dreamstime.com

ILLUSTRATIONS

The Horse Indians

Contents

#4.
"Chief Buffalo Horn"
Courtesy Idaho State
Historical Society

#5.
"Shoshoni-Bannock
Warriors"
Courtesy Idaho State
Historical Society

8

Acknowledgements

My deepest thanks to Teresa, owner of Azusa Publishing, L.L.C., in Denver, Colorado for all of the wonderful iconic Indian post cards she has graciously allowed me to use in this text. The pictures really make the book in my estimation. Her website and ad for gorgeous authentic Indian postcards is in the back of the book. I highly recommend that you try her web site.

I would like to thank the Smithsonian Institute for the Chief Washakie village photograph and also the Library of Congress for the excellent ancient wickiup photo.

I would also like to thank my Shoshone-Bannock Indian friend, Rosemary Devinney for answering my questions about her people, every time I call her. Rosemary is the Curator of the Fort Hall Shoshone-Bannock Museum.

I would like to thank Bonnie Fitzpatrick (*Designer*) for her formatting and graphic design.

My thanks go out to Len Sodenkamp, especially drawing his interpretation of the "Buffalo Hunter on Horseback."

I would like to thank the Wal-Mart Photo staff for their processing of pictures and to my friends at Fed-ex Office for their help in preparation.

#6. Wickiup
Courtesy Library of Congress

#7. Teepee
Courtesy Azusa Publishing Company, LLC

Forward

Prehistoric ancestors of the Shoshoni crossed through the Bering Straits over the land bridge and entered Alaska onto the American Continent thousands of years ago. They migrated into present day Canada and into America.

Early on the Northern Shoshoni tribes were "Walking Shoshonis" and traveled everywhere on foot. Legend tells us that five bands of Shoshoni Indians split from the Eastern Shoshoni tribe at Wind River, in what is now Wyoming, and migrated south, circa 1500.

Historical record places Comanche Indians in New Mexico in the early 16th Century. The Comanches were Shoshoni Indians of the Southern Plains. They had migrated south, leaving Shoshoni country around 1500, moving into what is now Colorado, Nebraska, Kansas, and Oklahoma; continuing south they chose the region, now known as Texas, to lodge and dwell. They settled around the headwaters of the Brazos, Cimarron, Canadian and Red Rivers.

Comanche territory known as "Comancheria," covered a large area of Colorado, Kansas, New Mexico, Oklahoma and Texas. The Comanche Indians maintained their territory, keeping strangers and their enemies out and guarded it like a dynasty. Being expert horsemen and fierce competitors, they were truly Lords of the Plains. They defeated all enemy challengers.

The Apache Indians raided the Spanish colonists in the 1500's, stealing horses. The Comanche slipped in at night and stole horses from the Apache, an act of bravery. It was their way of counting coup. They became Horse and Buffalo Indians of the Southern Plains. Becoming horse-mounted, the Comanche made raids on the Spanish haciendas of Mexican colonists in New Mexico, Texas and Mexico. More horses were taken after the Pueblo Revolt.

The Comanche Indians were skilled warriors, horsemen and breeders of horses. It is reported that the Comanche Indians drove possibly, 2,000 head of horses north to their northern counter-parts, circa 1700 A.D. The Wind River and Boise River Shoshoni Indians hosted trade fairs at their Trade Centers and horses were diffused to the tribes of the Northwest. The first time the Blackfeet ever saw horses, was when the Shoshoni rode into their village to attack them in 1730. The Comanche Horse Indians supplied the Indian tribes of the Northwest with horses.

Comanche warriors would fight anyone in their path, such as the Spanish and Mexican Armies, the U.S. Army, the Texas Rangers and other Indian tribes. They prevented Spanish expansion in Texas. The Comanche Indians fought the white man for 150 years before admitting defeat and moving onto the reservation.

#8. Cheyenne Chieftain
Courtesy Azusa Publishing Company, LLC

Chapter One
Migration

Constant raids by the powerful Sioux Indians in Canada and North America forced the Shoshoni Indians onto the Plains. The mighty Blackfeet braves attacked the Shoshoni people and pushed them farther west.

The Northern Shoshoni Indians withdrew into the Plateau and the Great Basin regions of the Rocky Mountains known as present day central Idaho. The climate was suitable and relatively mild except for intense summer heat and heavy snowfall. Natural resources of these regions were rich and teemed with fish, flora and fauna to comfortably sustain them in the northern Great Basin and Plateau cultural regions.

Shoshonis called themselves "Newe or numunuh," meaning "the people" or the "human beings." When white men saw the Bannock, Paiute and Shoshoni women digging roots, they called them "Digger Indians."

The husband's extended family lived in the territory of the tribe of his father. Authority and possessions were passed down through the father's line. The Shoshoni Indians followed the custom of arraigned marriages. Male warriors died in combat and lived more strenuous lives than the females. Because there were larger populations of women in the band, they practiced polygamy in marriage. As a result, many Plains Indian tribes practiced polygamy, which was the act of having more than one husband or wife.

A man who married an Indian bride took her younger sisters for wives, also and the family dwelled in the same lodge. Non-related wives had to live in separate lodges. If a woman desired more than one husband, she could marry her husband's younger brother.

Shoshonis were made up of bands, rather than clans. Shoshoni families banded together as an extended family of two or three generations that lived and traveled in one band. An autonomous composite group was also referred to as a band. Most bands had a band chief. When family bands joined in a village or winter camp, they usually had a head chief, band chief or headman, social director of ceremonies, dances, festivals, hunts and war.

Head-chief was the head man, or leader who might have served as hunt or war leader. Indian agents picked one man as head man to represent the whole tribe, translated into English as the word "chief" invented by the white man. The word chief designated authority in books written about Indians in English.

Prior to the horse, Shoshoni bands were pedestrian or "walking Indians." As horse-mounted buffalo hunters they were classified as "Plains Indians."

They were a breed of Shoshoni that spoke similar dialects of the Uto-Aztecan (Shoshonean) language speaking family, known as numic speakers akin to the Bannock, Paiute and Ute tribes in the same language stock. Shoshonean covers a widespread language family who ranged mainly over California, Colorado, Idaho, Nevada, Oregon, Utah and Wyoming, including the Arizonan Hopi and the Mexican Aztec Indians. Comanche Indians spoke the same language as the Shoshoni Indians, but the dialect varied over time.

In the Comanche language, vowels are pronounced phonetically, like ay, ee, ii, oh and ou. Consonants are spoken like English. The bilabial fricative is like a v, but the sound is produced with the lips held together instead of putting the upper teeth over the lower lip. A flapped r is one produced when the tongue is placed against the roof of the mouth and

14

#9. Mining & Industrial Exposition,
Southern Ute Indians, Denver, Colorado
Courtesy Azusa Publishing Company, LLC

#10. The Treaty of Laramie, Wyoming Territory-Cheyenne and Lakota
Chiefs, (left to right) Spotted Tail, Roman-Nose, One-Old-Man-Afraid-of-
His-Horses, Horn, Whistling Elk, Pipe and Slow Bull.
Courtesy Azusa Publishing Company, LLC

15

quickly let drop while forming the r. A dental t is formed by placing the tongue gainst the upper teeth instead of the fore-palate. The Comanche dialect is made up of different symbols for various short vowel sounds. A colon after a vowel (:) signifies that it is prolonged and drawn out. A single quotation mark (') means a glottal stop.

No written language existed in the beginning. Indians carved elaborate petro-glyphs in caves, on rock walls, boulders and flat stones. Maps, historic accounts and murals were etched in stone and depicted events, recorded in time. Messages on bark were left along the trail. Various tribes used universal "sign language" to communicate, if there was no interpreter. The Bannock, Paiute and Shoshoni tribes were called Snake Indians. Neighboring tribes referred to them using sign language in a slithering hand motion to describe how the Shoshoni disappeared behind rocks like snakes.

Young braves were taught early to hunt for food using bow and arrows. When they reached puberty, the braves exhibited their manhood on horseback with the bow, lance and shield. The braves or maidens began their vision quest before the age of twelve at puberty. Braves experienced the rite-of-passage, a personal vigil in becoming a man, to receive his vision quest. Vision quests were not always successful. The experience had to be real. The Shoshoni maiden underwent a similar experience in becoming a woman.

The boy or girl normally went out in nature, alone in the wild, where he or she stayed three or four days until he received his vision and sometimes used his religion and hallucinogens, such as mescal or peyote in order to produce such a vision. Each fasted and prayed to seek the desired revelation.

Self-purification in sweat baths, inhaling the smoke of the sweet grass or sage, personal sacrifice induced purity. The vision quest was a religious ordeal conducted in nature. Each candidate fasted in the wild for several days of isolation before experiencing their supernatural vision.

Animals or birds in nature served as their totem. When a young man or woman received a spiritual revelation or a supernatural vision in the form of a buffalo, eagle, raven or wolf spirit, it became the young brave's spirit guide through life that would give the seeker a new name, medicine or powers. He could choose a new name at this time, like Man-Afraid-of-His-Horses. A feather or claw of the animal might have been placed in his medicine bundle.

After a successful vision quest, the Comanche brave was expected to count coup, a way of proving manhood. "Coup," in French means touch. Counting coup in the eyes of the Plains Indians was executed by a brave act to show victory over the enemy and prove bravery.

To prove his valor and count coup a brave had to either run or ride up to touch the enemy with his hand, a stick or riding quirt to show courage. To enter an enemy camp at night and take horses was another means of counting coup for every horse stolen. Besides taking coup, horses made up wealth. It was considered a braver act to kill an enemy warrior up close using a tomahawk than to shoot him with an arrow and count coup.

The next major challenge was his first hunt and war trail. After he went to battle, he was considered a warrior. A young brave was expected to have a history of success on the battlefield to qualify for marriage.

Western Shoshoni bands were named for their dwelling places, such as the Boise, Bruneau and the Weiser River Shoshonis. The Boise and Bruneau River Shoshoni intermarried over time, becoming intermixed as one band. Northern Paiute and Western Shoshoni dwelled in south and western present day Idaho. Bannock Indians dwelled in central (what is now Idaho) east to the Fort Hall region and intermarried with the Fort Hall Shoshoni creating the Shoshoni-Bannock people. The Bear River Shoshoni lived southeast of Fort Hall and the Salmon River Shoshonis dwelled north central.

The Shoshoni Indians were a "hunting and gathering society." The men hunted and defended the band, while the women foraged for seeds, nuts and berries, tanned the hides, cooked and cared for the children.

The communal hunts encompassed everything from grasshoppers to buffalo. The whole band was involved and they all profited from the hunt. The hunt often ended with celebration and dance festivities. Communal drives were used to entrap antelope, buffalo, deer, rabbit and sage hen and an effective method to capture prey.

The Shoshoni people held communal grasshopper drives and corralled insects. They encircled the bugs and drove them into netting in the center to trap them. Grasshoppers were ground into a paste in mortars or flour to make grasshopper bread. Edible grasshoppers and crickets, containing high amounts of protein were roasted.

Drives for antelope were a communal activity. Herds of antelope ranged into the hundreds. The antelope's speed was its defense from predators being able to run instantly. Antelope were caught in corrals similar to buffalo. In smaller communal antelope drives, the Indians surrounded the antelope, and moved inward until the animal was ensnared. In a larger drives, the Indians spread out in a huge circle and completely surrounded the herd and drove the antelope between lanes of brush and rocks into the catching corral. The Shoshonis slaughtered what they needed and freed the rest.

Another means to hunt antelope was by a shaman, who planned the hunt. The Shaman used his magic to entice the pronghorn using

#11.Washakie, Chief of the Wind and Green River Shoshoni
Courtesy Azusa Publishing Company LLC

trickery to lure the antelope to come to him. He hid in the sagebrush and held a bright colored cloth tied to a long stick, high in the air. As he slowly waved the flag back and forth, the curious antelope approached him. The animal was then easily shot with bow and arrows.

A different way of hunting antelope also involved a medicine man. Antelope corrals were built and the shaman fashioned an antelope decoy of reeds and played a crude musical instrument that emitted an eerie sound that charmed the animal to become curios and approach him. He also chanted songs to entice the antelope into the corral. They believed this was the shaman's magic. If the trap was empty, the Indians circled the herd and drove them into the corral to be slaughtered. The meat was shared by the whole band. An Antelope Festival followed the hunt with much festivity.

Northern Shoshoni Indians hunted buffalo on foot and after the horse were called "walking Indians." The Buffalo jump was an unusual technique of hunting used by the Northern Shoshoni. Lanes were built on a plateau with rock barriers along the sides forming a corridor. When the herd grazed near the cliff; a medicine man whooped and waved a blanket or lit a brush fire causing the herd to spook and stampede over the edge. Buffalo wounded from the fall, were put out of their misery with their spears, tomahawks and war-clubs. Meat was separated from the hides in kill-sites, processing stations, at the base of the cliff, where they were butchered. Later, the warriors brought hides to be stretched and scraped.

A buffalo corral was constructed in a V shape, on a down slope. The shaman crawled among the herd, under a buffalo robe and bleated to mimic a baby buffalo as he crawled. Buffalo have poor eyesight and the dumb animal followed the shaman into the corral to be trapped and shot.

The Northern Shoshoni lived in fear of the fierce Sioux and Ute Indian raids. The horse-mounted Ute marauders rode in and ambushed

#12. Eastern Shoshoni Village of Shoshoni Chief Washakie
Courtesy Smithsonian Institute

#13. Bannock Indians, Allies of the Shoshoni People
Courtesy Azusa Publishing Company, LLC

their camps without sentries to capture women and children for trade with the Spanish after 1500 A.D. The captives were sold to Spanish colonists. An ancient Indian trail, later known as the Old Spanish Trail was used by the Ute traders during the slave trade in the 1600's to traffic slaves and stolen horses.

With no written record, stories come from oral tradition from the Shoshoni tribe. They do not remember when the Comanche left, but legend relates how five bands of Shoshonis split from the Eastern Shoshoni tribe at Wind River, in now Wyoming, and migrated south to northern Texas, circa 1500. Southern Shoshonis that left became known as Comanche Indians.

One account was told about how the Comanche departed from the Eastern Shoshoni tribe. A band of Shoshonis traveling south were startled by the eerie howl of a timber wolf nearby. Some in the party counted the wolf cry as a sign or bad omen. The chief and half of the band turned around and went back. The rest of the band chose a new head man and continued on their journey, destined to migrate southward and become the Comanche Indians.

One tale told of the Comanche-Shoshone split occurred with children playing. In the midst of the action as they played a kicking game; a chief's son was kicked too hard in the stomach and died. West camp had a head chief and mourned through the night, while the other chief and the east camp was silent. The ailing chief asked a crier to announce a big battle for the two sides to fight for revenge to settle the question of the death. Warriors from the east camp mounted their horses, intending to run away. The warriors lined up on both sides. It was then that the chief was overcome with grief and spoke; he wept and begged them to call off the fighting. One chief decided to move west, the other north.

Many stories have been passed down over time to explain how the Comanche-Shoshoni division occurred. One tale from legend was told of how two bands of Shoshoni Indians joined together to go form a hunting party and killed a bear. An argument arose over whose arrow had actually killed the bruin and how to divide it. A brave from each band claimed the victory; one of the two bands moved away, settling the argument.

According to Comanche legend, a band of pedestrian Eastern Shoshoni Indians separated from the Wind River band and walked out of present day Wyoming, circa 1500 A.D. They reappeared in Taos, New Mexico, known as Comanche Indians 200 years later. This saga is a fictional scenario based on fact to describe how the Comanche Indians reached Texas.

In the spring, around 1500 A.D., the family bands prepared for the extended journey. The long procession moved out anticipating their journey. A long caravan of Shoshoni people began the trek on foot, traveling eastward. Young women toted their babies (papooses) in cradleboards on their backs. Others packed goods on their backs or used dogs, as beasts of burden, to haul moderate loads by travois along the Snake River toward the rising sun. This was the only means to transport goods for hundreds of years. Comanche Indians were recorded using dogs for this means as early as 1540.

Domestic dogs were also kept as family pets, watchdogs and in some cases for hunting. The Shoshoni Indians honored the dog; they were too proud and abstained from eating dog meat. The Arapaho and Cheyenne Indian Tribes however ate the meat of young, tender puppies; a custom looked down on by the Shoshoni people. Later on, Comanches ate dog meat.

The legend was told of how they left the Wind River region (present day Wyoming) and journeyed eastward across Colorado for many sleeps

23

before reaching Nebraska, along the Platte River in Pawnee country.

The Shoshoni Indians had formed a powerful buffalo hunting society and their culture centered on the buffalo. The bands of Shoshoni were nomads, since they followed the movements of the buffalo herds by the weather and season. They moved their villages with the annual bison migration. The buffalo provided the much needed meat, skins, clothing, moccasins, horns, tools and teepee coverings. Their diet was predominately buffalo meat, an excellent staple, supplemented with roots and berries.

The region was rich with buffalo and they moved with the woolly beasts. For many moons (months), they took advantage of the number of buffalo that were there. The Shoshoni buffalo eaters or "k'ut-sun-de-kas" migrated on foot, and followed the buffalo as the herds moved south. Five bands made up of about 100 Shoshonis were led by a head man.

Shoshoni hunted bear, deer, elk, rabbit, wolf and other mammals and birds for food, in addition to buffalo. The families ate of the rich buffalo meat and tanned the hides. They slowly moved across Kansas into the Oklahoma panhandle following the ranging buffalo, south as they grazed. Their families trailed behind with goods on their backs, while dogs pulled loads on travois.

The hypothesis has been proven that tribes always on the move did not have time to make baskets and pottery. More sedentary peoples dwelled in villages and were more apt to craft basketry and earthenware. They did not make baskets and pots, but attained them from other tribes.

Men, women and children in the caravan followed the buffalo and trekked methodically southward. The long line moved from Oklahoma and finally reached the northern region of Texas. Over the years, the Shoshoni Comanche Indians ranged from the Platte Valley of Nebraska into the present day northern Texas panhandle.

Chapter Two
Hunting Buffalo

It is theorized that after the last Ice Age corridors opened up due to the melting of the ice sheets across Siberia and abundant herds of bison crossed the Bering Straits from Eurasia into North American to populate America, from Mexico to Alaska. Early man entered the continent to follow migratory herds of buffalo that supplied meat, tents and clothing for them.

A much larger predecessor to the modern buffalo called the ancient bison (bison antiquus) was hunted by prehistoric peoples. It was a forerunner of the modern wood and plains bison.

In the summer of 1927, near Folsom, New Mexico a rancher discovered a fluted atlatl spearhead, with fossil ancient bison antiquus bones, circa 9,000 B.P., coined the Folsom point.

The Pleistocene atlatl was the weapon for hunting used by early man that preceded the bow and arrow. The atlatl was a device used to throw a spear using a flat wooden stick with a groove or peg to insert into the butt-end of a spear, which was thrust 40-50 yards to pierce a massive bison or mastodon. The ancient bison was hunted by prehistoric man on the continent with the atlatl.

From days of old until the present, buffalo herds multiplied, and flourished, sometimes blackening the prairie as far as the eye could see. The Great Plains covered the broad expanse of grassland, west of the Mississippi River and east of the Rocky Mountains in North America and southern Canada. The Great Plains region was the home of several Indian tribes and millions of bison. The buffalo population was estimated as high as 50,000,000 in the 18th century; their populations once covered half of the continent.

#14. Plainswoman, Horse & Travois
Courtesy Azusa Publishing Company, LLC

#15. Buffalo Herd in Yellowstone
Courtesy Nampa.net

Wild buffalo roamed the untamed wilderness between Canada in the Northwest, south into Mexico, and eastward along the Appalachian Mountains. There was an abundance of bison on the Snake River Plain westward into Oregon Territory to the base of the Blue Mountains before the turn of the 19th century. They began to disappear after that, due to over-kill and were reduced to less than 5,000,000 buffalo on the American Plains in 1860.

Tens of millions of indigenous buffalo once rumbled across miles of grassland on the Great Plains in pre-historic times and must have raised huge clouds of dust. Buffalo are grazing ruminants, a species of wild cow that fed on grasses, sedges, and occasionally berries and lichen. The wooly beasts ate grasses down so short that in a short time they had to migrate in order to reach other grasses. Buffalo drank from lakes, rivers or streams.

Buffalo provided warm robes (worn fur side out) for winter clothing and moccasins. Buffalo alone provided an industry. The Plains culture encompassed hunting buffalo, for centuries their life source. The buffalo was the largest land animal hunted by the Indians of the Plains and the life blood of the Plains Indian and was their sole living, supplying most of their needs.

The woodland buffalo is the world's largest cattle species. A male buffalo is a very large animal that can weigh over 2,000 pounds, while the cows could weigh from 700 to 900 pounds. Bulls reach seven feet in height and females reach five feet in height to the shoulder. Buffalo have a massive head, two short curved pointed horns, hump shoulders, cropped ears, abbreviated snout and wide-spread eyes with a woolly coat on their head, shaggy hair on the belly, smaller hind quarters, and short tail with a tuft of hair on the tip. Buffalo have a shaggy coat in winter and a lighter summer coat.

#16. "Buffalo Pair"
Courtesy Nampa.net

#17. White Buffalo
Courtesy Dreamstime.com

Both bull and cow buffalo have horns; only male bison have horns and not the cows. Despite their size, buffalo can run as fast as forty miles per hour.

Buffalo usually ranged in smaller herds of same sex, but grazed in massive mixed herds in the summer, during mating season. Bulls banded together, separate from cows, by sex in bachelor herds, except at breeding time, which allowed bulls, cows and calves in the mixed herd. Mixed herds consisted of bulls, cows and calves, a species of wild cattle of family bovidae.

Female buffalo formed smaller maternal herds that included male and female offspring. Males left the herd around three years of age to roam alone or join a bachelor herd and banded together in small herds. The sexes did not mix until summer, when they formed massive herds that fed on annual grasses during mating season. Their movement was referred to as the seasonal round.

Buffalo are polygamous during mating season. Buffalo were quite gregarious. Their age created a hierarchy. Older bison were the more dominant. Larger males tended to be dominant bulls. Dominant males passed on their dominance by breeding early in the season and were most fertile. A dominant bull maintained his harem in season and was most mated within the first two to three weeks.

A bull tended his estrous cow and followed her around until she accepted him. Submissive males mated with any estrous cow, not mated. He stood and shielded her eyes from a challenging bull, whose bellow was heard three miles away; if the challenger bellowed, the tending bull answered. Bulls fought each other for mating rites to breed the cows and lost as much as 200 pounds during mating season, with little time to graze.

The Plains Indians believed that buffaloes were created just for the Indian people and that the buffalo were sacred. It completed their life

#18.
Buffalo Hunter
on Horseback
Courtesy Len Sodenkamp,
Boise Artist

19.
"Young Buffalo"
Author Photo

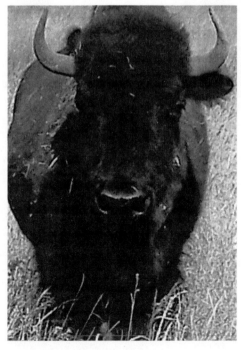

style. Their whole world centered around the buffalo. Shoshonis depended on the buffalo for food, shelter and clothing and other by-products.

The Snake Indians crafted fine bows of Cedar, Juniper, Oak, Osage or Yew. Arrows were made of the same or similar materials. Bow strings were produced from animal sinew. A shaft was heated , straightened, smoothed and polished for an arrow. Indians flint knapped (flaked) arrowheads from obsidian, or chert and inserted them into a slit at the shaft end, glued with pitch and wrapped with sinew. Eagle, hawk or similar feathers were used to fletch an arrow. Weapons were covered with animal skins, decorated with glass beads and dyed porcupine quills; rattlesnake was a favorite skin used. The bow and arrows they fashioned were admired by other tribes. Men were taught to hunt game, early with bows and arrows.

Shoshoni hunted buffalo in small hunting parties and sent scouts to locate the roving bison herds on foot in the wild for the hunt; they had to approach the herd from downwind to avoid a stampede. Buffalo have poor eyesight, but a keen sense of smell. It was possible to be trampled by stampeding bison and dangerous to attempt to hunt buffalo alone.

Hunters encountered massive herds of buffalo at times, numbering in the hundreds; the braves hunted buffalo to feed his extended family. They usually had a hunt leader and took down buffalo using bow and arrows. Even though Indians killed their share of buffalo, they conserved hunting sparingly. The populations didn't diminish greatly, until after the white man came. Hunting from smaller herds caused them to drift away. The buffalo provided the Indian with plenty of meat and raiment.

Buffalo herds offered some security against predators. Wolves often followed the herds and attacked the shaggy beasts in packs and often preyed on the young and weak buffalo. The buffalo were accustomed to

#20. "American Buffalo"
Author Photo

#21 "Lone Buffalo Grazing"
Courtesy Nampa.net

lone wolves being in the vicinity, that were not a great danger to them.

Knowing this, an Indian hunter, hidden under a wolf skin, crawled among the bison and could get a good shot with his bow and arrow. The Indian tradition was to first kill a buffalo and the heart was then cut out and eaten raw, in order to gain its power.

When early man first used fire to cook and to heat their dwellings is not certain. Fire was used in hunting and warfare and in forests by some tribes to remove dead grasses and underbrush. In battle, Indians lit brush fires as the wind blew toward the enemy as a deterrent.

Shoshoni Indians were skilled buffalo hunters. The female bison were taken in late autumn, before winter so the hides could be made into warm robes before the cold season. They preferred that the animals be taken in late autumn because their fur was longer then.

In the cold of winter, with deep snows and howling headwinds, the roving bison found refuge in wooded valleys and hilly terrain using them for wind breaks. Bison wintered in timber where the snow was shallow. They used their scruffy coarse fur faces and horns to brush away the snow to make a clearing to lie down. Heavy snow slowed the buffalo, to become easy targets for Indian hunter's arrows. Snow shoes were often worn on these occasions.

Bison were sometimes caught in a flash flood and drowned as they had poor eyesight and poor judgment; they ventured out onto snow covered icy rivers. The ice gave way and they drowned under breaking ice.

Women did the cooking and preparation. The majority of the red meat that they ate was from the buffalo. They wasted very little and the relished meat that was eaten fresh or jerked. Bison meat was cut in strips, dried and jerked in the sun over a rack for jerky.

Jerky was pounded into a powder in the mortar and pestle, combined with fat and berries and made into pemmican cakes or placed in skin bags for later. The buffalo were so plentiful that there was enough surplus meat to be stored to last the winter. They were successful hunters and provided ample amounts of food for their people.

One method of cooking buffalo meat occurred by using red-hot stones from a fire, which were put into pitch lined baskets filled with water. As the water simmered, meat was added. Meat was also cooked in clay vessels, a paunch (belly of an animal and its contents) or in a pit. Water was boiled in a skin held with four stakes in the ground and hot rocks added to provide heat. The Shoshoni were mobile, so baskets and pots were procured through trade.

Fresh meat was cooked with wild caraway, celery, parsnip, Indian potatoes, and other wild vegetables added to the water to make stew. Meat was broiled on spits over the fire or on a green willow stick (skewer). Three slender flat rocks (fire dogs) supported a pot cooking over a fire.

Hides were stretched out by driving pegs into the ground in a perimeter. Women staked the skins and scraped the hides to remove all of the flesh and fat with stone hide-scrapers. Skins were then tanned by rubbing a portion of buffalo brain solution into the hides to process the fleshed skins.

The hides were then processed in warm water and hung from a tree branch about shoulder level. They were scraped again to give them flexibility. Animal skins were chewed, pounded in mortars, kneaded and stretched to make them more pliable. The hump was removed and the skin sewn up. Bull hides were not tanned, but used for hard moccasin soles and belts.

Indian women processed buckskin using a different procedure, not tanned and used a smoking technique to cure the hides, dug a pit and started a fire with white cedar and stretched the skin over bent green willows that hung over the fire, making sure the flames did not blaze up and ruin the skin. The smoking process made the finished product soft and supple and was used in women's yellow-clothing. It was easily cut, sewed, washed and dyed red or yellow, using a solution of boiled wild peach or red oak bark.

Elk was also an excellent food source. Elk skin processed hides were soft, making good moccasins and excellent dresses. The Indian conserved using every part of the animal with little waste. Women donned dresses and jackets of elk and used elk teeth to decorate their clothing. Moose were hunted for the meat, hides, bone and horn. The hides made warm clothing and leather moccasins that were more soft and supple than buffalo leather. Deer and elk were plentiful and a band shared the kill. Antelope, bear, beaver, buffalo, deer, elk, fox, rabbit and wolf fur made good robes. The soft fur of the antelope was used to wrap Indian babies.

Besides their other work women sewed all of the clothing for the whole family from soft deerskin, using stone or bone awls burins, bone eye needles and sinew. Deerskin clothing was standard on the Plains and was used for moccasins. Antlers were made into tools. The sinew was used to bind arrowheads to the arrow shafts and for sewing. Fringed deerskin or trade-cloth dresses made dresses with porcupine quill or tobacco can lid cone decor with a belt, or just skirts, exposing the breasts in the heat of summer and deer skin leggings were worn from the moccasins to the knees. Innocent children ran naked until they were five.

Men wore deerskin war-shirts (tunics), breech clouts (loin cloths), and moccasins. Leggings were fringed from the hips to the ankles past the seams. Decorated leggings were of beadwork, quillwork or with painted designs.

Moccasins were crafted by different methods. A rare Plains Indian moccasin type was the hock moccasin, formed from the sheath of the hock section of the foreleg of the deer or buffalo, made from one piece, hair on the inside. The top was sewn shut and fitted with a thong to tie the top.

The Freemont style moccasin used three pieces of leather from the upper leg sheath of the deer, formed into moccasins. Soft soles were utilized for winter ware and hard soles were worn in the summer.

"Tipi," is a Lakota Sioux word for a place where one lives. The Plains teepee (tipi) was a large tent erected quickly, stretched over a number of lodge poles on a conical shaped framework, open near the top, to vent the smoke.

The buffalo skins were sewn together with sinew to make teepee coverings anchored with rocks. Hides, matting or robes made up the flooring. Eight to twenty buffalo skins covered a teepee. A teepee was 15 feet in diameter, collapsible to transport and easy to set up or break down.

Their women could use the horse to pull a travois loaded with teepee hide coverings, camp equipment, goods, utilities and infants. They made camp near water and normally near game. On the hunt, tepees were situated in the round. Encampments were usually circular for protection.

The Buffalo Tongue Ceremony was more a feast, where the host swore an oath. He or the medicine man lit the pipe and blew puffs of smoke first to the sun and second to the earth. He then blew smoke in all four directions. When he was done, the host passed the pipe. After all had smoked, a woman was called to serve the tongues. All of the women gave a cry of yi, yi, yi, yi, yi, and applause before the buffalo tongues were served.

The Buffalo Utility

Buffalo-	clan symbol, totem
Bladder-	medicine bags, quill & sinew pouches
Bones-	game dice, awls, burins & needles
Brains-	to cure hides, robes
Buckskin-	moccasins, shirts, pouches, quivers
Buffalo chip-	fuel for fires, signals
Ears-	ornamentation
Entrails-	heart, gizzard & liver eaten
Flesh-	meat, jerky, pemmican, & ribs
Fur-	blankets, robes
Hair-	braided rope, bridals halters
Hides-	teepee covering, robes, moccasins
Hind leg-	pre-shaped moccasins & boots
Hooves-	glue, rattles
Horns-	cups, ladles, spoons
Meat-	food, jerky, pemmican
Muscle-	bows, thread, sinew
Rawhide-	clothing, drums, saddles, stirrups
Scalp and horns-	headdress, Sun Dance
Scrotum-	rattles
Shoulder blade-	hoe
Skin-	clothing, moccasins, teepees
Sinew-	arrows, sewing, binding
Skull-	Sun Dance, sacred, prayer
Stomach-	buckets, cooking vessel
Tail-	whips, medicine switch, fly brush
Teeth-	necklaces, ornaments
Tongue-	good meat

#22. "Spanish Mustang"
Photo courtesy www.aaanativearts.com

Chapter Three
Spanish Mustangs

Christopher Columbus brought horses to the American continent and found them useful in 1495 to attack a warring tribe. He recommended that horses be on board sailing vessels bound for America from Spain.

Spanish Conquistador, Hernan Cortez sailed from Cuba with a flotilla of 10 galleons, 600 soldier, 18 horsemen, ten stallions and six mares on board. When he landed on the shore of the Gulf of Mexico in 1519, he brought the first modern horses to the "New World."

The Spanish Europeans continued to bring horses on their voyages. Spanish Galleons brought Appaloosa, Arabian, Tartar horses and Spanish Mustangs as cargo to the Mexican shores for the Army and colonists. Horses were in every shipment from Spain. Spanish galleons hauled horses on every voyage to the Coast of Mexico, after that.

Hernan Cortez conquered Mexico's Aztec empire. Montezuma believed Cortez to be their god, Quetzalcoatl (the plumed serpent returned), perhaps thinking horse and rider to be one beast.

The Ute tribe stole horses from the Spanish in the 1500's during night raids. Cortez made slaves of horse thieves that he caught among the Ute Indians and forced them to work his gold mines.

In 1540, Coronado made an expedition onto the Southern Plains and stormed the American southwest. He arrived in the southwest with horses and superior modern weaponry and overpowered the Indians with their fire power. The Spanish intruders forced them to be subservient. The Indians were exploited. Cruel Spaniards whipped, enslaved and hanged the Indians. Spanish armies massacred the Pueblo village of Tiguex on the Rio Grande River when they rebelled.

#23. Pueblo House
Courtesy Legends of America.com

#24. Mesa Verde Cliff Dwellers
Author Photo

Coronado left the Pueblos and withdrew to New Spain (which was Central America, Mexico and the Southwest). There was 40 years of peace. They were followed by Spanish colonists, who landed on the Pacific Coast of Mexico and California.

Legend repeats that when the Ute Indians first saw horses, they called horses, "big dogs." Utes were the first American Indian tribe to own horses. The warriors entered into slave trade with the Spanish in the mid 1600s. With the horse and the element of surprise the ruthless Ute braves took slaves from unguarded Shoshoni and other Plains Indian's villages.

Apache and Ute Indians raided the Pueblos and Spanish colonists in the 1600's continually stealing horses. As Apache Indians stole horses from the colonists, the Comanches went on the war trail and raided Apache camps to steal horses at night, right out from under the Apaches' noses.

Spanish colonists in the American Southwest built their haciendas and ranchos using adobe bricks, made of clay (dug from river mud) and straw and dried in the sun. The colonists had nice ranches and plenty of horses.

When they first fought the Ute Indians, these Shoshoni Indians came to be referred to as "Komantcia," or enemy, literally "anyone who wants to fight me all the time;" the Spanish learned the name from the Ute Indians and identified them as "Comanche Indians." The Arapaho, Cheyenne and Kiowa Indians that fought the Ute were called Komantcia also. This is how the Shoshonis came to be called the Comanche Indians.

The Anasazi people were an ancient forerunner of the modern Pueblo Indians, who have been in place for a long period of time. They lived in terraced dwellings with flat roofs. The villages were multi storied communal apartments they reached with ladders that could be pulled up for their protection. Adjoining houses were made of adobe or stone, nestled against cliffs under stone overhangs or were free standing.

New Mexico was colonized by the Spanish in 1598. Juan de Onate pressed north in search of gold along the Rio Grande River and discovered the Pueblo Indians and settled among them. This region contained villages of the Pueblo Indian farmers, who worked the rich soil. His armies conquered and enslaved them. If the Indians fled, the Pueblos were surrounded by hostile Indians who would also enslave them and they had no place to run.

Onate observed the Plains Apaches along the Canadian River. He made serfs of the Indios to work their own land by force. Onate brought 7,000 head of cattle from Mexico. There was unrest among the Pueblos.

The merciless Spaniards treated the Pueblo Indians very cruelly and forcibly proselytized them to accept Roman Catholicism. In 1629, the Zuni Indians revolted against Spanish rule in their village. The Spaniards in the southwest forced the western pueblos of the Acoma, Hopi, and Zuni Indians to accept Catholic missionaries, in 1633.

Spaniards were cruel taskmasters of the Pueblo Indians. They were forced to work as common serfs in the Pueblos. The ruthless Spaniards did not allow the Indians to ride or own horses, so Spanish vaqueros (cowboys) worked the cattle. This kept the Indians from escaping on horseback and limited their movement. The Spanish hoarded the horses, but still lost stock to coyotes, cougars, eagles and hostile Indians.

The Spaniards treated these Indians very poorly and sometimes they were killed. Slaves were made to build corrals and stables. Beleaguered slaves were forced to herd sheep and goats, while the boys were made to feed and water the horses and clean stables. The Navajos grew weary of tending the animals day and night. The Navajos were getting restless.

The abuse of Indian slaves continued until around 1680, when the enslaved Navajos rebelled. The New Mexico Indian tribes rose up and overthrew the Spanish rule during the "Pueblo Revolt" and drove the Spanish colonists, priests and soldiers out. Many of the Spaniards were killed. The Spanish colonists retreated, fled the country, and left thousands of cattle, horses and sheep behind. Indians raided the ranchos and stole horses.

Many thousands of Spanish mustangs broke loose and escaped from the colonists' ranches. For the first time, wild (feral) horses roamed free on the desert of the Southern Plains. Hundreds of roving family bands of feral horses were caught and broken. Horses were free and Indians garnered many mustangs and other breeds at that time, later called the "American Mustangs."

Comanche Indians acquired the horse in 1680 and earlier, having stolen horses from the Apaches before. The Comanche Indians continued to raid for horses, as did the Apache, and Ute Indians, who stormed Spanish Colonists' haciendas in New Mexico for horses.

In 1716, the Spanish Army attacked a Comanche camp north of Santa Fe. The soldiers captured prisoners, who were sold into slavery.

In 1719, Comanche Indians made the first recorded raids for horses on Spanish settlements along the Rio Grande River. The Apache Indians also raided the Spanish settlements for horses. Comanche horsemen were equipped to raid the Spanish settlements deep into the heart of Mexico.

Comanche Indians stole horses and became the third American Indian tribe, following the Ute and Apache Indians to own horses. The Comanches went on to provide horses to most all of the Indians in the Pacific Northwest.

While the Comanche Indians migrated south into present day northern Texas, they impacted the Apache Indians. The Jicarilla Apache

#25. Navajo Hogan & Corral
Author Photo

#26. "Navajo Woman Herding Sheep"
Author Photo

#27. Navajo Blanket Weaver
Courtesy Azusa Publishing Company, LLC

#28. Horse-mounted Navajos
Courtesy Azusa Publishing Company, LLC

#29.
Warrior of the Navajo
Courtesy Azusa Publishing
Company, LLC

#30.
Navajo Warrior Strings Bow"
Courtesy Azusa Publishing
Company, LLC

Indians were peaceful buffalo hunters and farmers, who may have learned about agriculture from the Pueblo Indians. These Apaches stayed in one location to grow beans, corn and squash. Comanche war parties took advantage of their peaceful nature and raided them and dominated the other tribes on the High Plains.

The Comanche had the horse after the Ute and Apache Indians, but became the most expert horsemen and the fiercest warriors of any tribe on the Southern Plains. The Comanche tribe has been acclaimed the finest horsemen of all of the American Indians. Captain Randolph Marcy of the U.S. Army proclaimed the Comanche Indians to be the most expert horsemen in the world. George Catlin corroborated views. "In racing and riding," George Catlin agreed, "they are not equaled by any other Indians on the continent."

The coming of the horse caused the biggest transformation in the lives of the American Indian, ever. The Sioux Indian tribe mastered the horse in war fare and hunting, but the Comanche seemed to top them all.

The Comanche warriors skirmished with the Apaches and managed to push them back and triumphed over them using newly acquired firearms. The fierce Comanche, on the warpath, made night-raids on the Jicarilla and Mescalero Apache Indians in northern Texas to steal their horses and stock.

With the horse they destroyed their camps and took captives of the Apache people. The Comanche marauders raided the Apache encampments continually and pushed them off their lands. Jicarilla Apaches were forced off of their lands by repeated Comanche and Ute Indian raids.

They had driven the Apaches out of Texas and now owned the land as their territory. It would come to be known as Comancheria. The Apaches fled to the mountains and into Mexico. The Comanches gained the horse and adopted a new way of life. With the horse they no longer had to trek everywhere that they went. They had horses to ride and to haul their goods.

The Spanish militia was the first intruder that the Comanches fought in their territory. Spanish explorer, Sieur do La Sill and his entourage met the Comanche Indians at their camp, as early as 1687, near the Trinity River. The Spanish colonists returned to New Mexico twelve years after the Pueblo Revolt. They re-established Santa Fe as the colony's capital in 1692.

The horse drastically changed their way of hunting and warfare. "The Horse and Indian Era," circa 1700-1875 allowed the American Indian the freedom of movement to travel great distances to hunt buffalo and raid distant enemy camps. The Comanche made night raids on the ranchos to steal horses and mules, building up their herds with Spanish horses.

The first raids by Comanche braves were recorded in New Mexico, from 1714-1720. In 1716, the Apache Indians fled into the mountains in fear of the fierce Comanche raiders, after the unruly Comanche warriors drove them out of Texas and south into Mexico.

As the Plains Indians got the horse, their whole style of hunting buffalo radically changed. The horse and buffalo were their salvation. The Indians had mobility to follow the herds or move in their seasonal rounds.

The government passed a law that nearly caused extinction of the American buffalo in 1871, by ordering all bison killed to force the Indians onto reservations. Bison were needlessly slaughtered by the thousands for their tongues and skins, the carcasses left to rot. By the late 1800s, buffalo had nearly died out. Never again would the Indian hunt the buffalo. Those days were gone. Most of the American bison now remain in Yellowstone.

Chapter Four
Horsemen

The Comanche stole horses early on from the Apaches and during the Pueblo Revolt. In the aftermath, thousands of wild horses that had broken loose roamed the desert. Comanche Indians regarded the horse as a gift from the gods and cherished them. They caught, broke, gentled and bred them.

These Indians became experience riders and could ride up on a feral horse and encircle its head with a lasso in the wild. The Comanche Indians not only used lassos to catch wild mustangs but became excellent horse handlers and breeders, also. The wild stallion was a powerful runner and could sometimes outdistance a pursuer or lead a wild herd.

The Comanche horsemen captured mustangs best in the cold of winter, when they were undernourished and too weak to resist and escape. During cold weather, wild horses were weaker, gaunter and starving. They had less resistance and gave in easier. These feral horses were easier to catch. When the Comanche braves came upon a mare with foal, the mother slowed down and stayed with its colt and two horses were caught. That way the colt could be raised to maturity.

Mustangs were taken from ranchos in northern Mexico and Texas ranches. They thought that horses were there for the taking. Comanche Indians amassed thousands of horses. Wealth in horses came in the number of head owned and the Comanche Indians collected large herds. It was not uncommon for a warrior to own 250 horses. A chief might have possessed a herd of 1,000 horses. Horses were gifted, traded, stolen or caught in the wild. Horses revolutionized the Indian life way changing their warfare, hunting, camp and seasonal moves.

Comanche horsemen also caught cayuses on a hot summer day. A wild bunch would graze on dry grasses and develop a thirst. Hot and sweaty, the wild mustangs would all gallop to the nearest water hole to drink. They would drink and drink until their bellies were full of water. When the horses attempted to run, being fat and sluggish, they were easy to catch. The horsemen would then ambush and capture them easily by surrounding them.

One method of catching horses, used by the Kiowa and Comanche was the corral method. The corral was built near a watering hole. The wild horses were driven into a v-shaped enclosure. When they were in the corral, the gate was then closed. Some corrals were built large enough to hold several hundred horses and used part of its natural surroundings for the enclosure.

The Indian technique of breaking horses was effective. Several Indians held the horse, using the lassoes; the feral horse was jerked off of its feet, hardly breathing. As the noose was tightened, restricting the horse's air supply, it lay on the ground, gasping for air; then the lasso was relaxed.

The lathered horse arose, weak and trembling, while its captor stroked its ears, forehead and nose. The mustang's captor then blew into its nostrils. Next, the brave bridled the horse, mounted it and rode away. The Comanche Indians had way with horses. Pack horses were broke in to haul loads using rocks to represent weight they would be carrying.

Indian saddles used were of two general types, the pad saddle and the frame saddle. The pad saddle was popular with the Comanche Indians, made of two leather pieces, sewn together and stuffed with either feathers or grass. The frame saddle of bison bone, wood or deer antler was light in weight. Wet rawhide was and stretched over it that was shrunk to size. It weighed about three pounds. The woman's saddle was of this type. Their saddles were adorned with saddle blankets and supple folds of buffalo hide. The saddles were attached by a single cinch of hair or hide. Hunting or warring Comanche warriors rode bareback. The bridle was made of horse hair, stitched about the horse's jaw. Bridles, saddles and pommels were heavily beaded.

Theories maintain that after the Pueblo Revolt horses were driven to various tribes from the Pueblos north, south, east and west and that the horse was traded west along the Coast of the Pacific Ocean.

When the Comanche Indians first saw horses, they thought that they were deities or "god dogs." Other stories of Indians were that the man and rider were conceived as one creature. The first time the Blackfeet Indians saw horses, was when a Shoshoni war party rode into their village to attack them in 1700; the Blackfeet were defeated and called horses "elk dogs."

Comanche horsemen had a huge surplus of horses and drove a large herd north to the Shoshonis. Legend tells how Comanche Indians drove hundreds of horses north to their Northern and Eastern Shoshoni counter-parts, indicating their point of origin and the Comanche's very beginnings, circa 1700. They supplied the first horses to the Nez Perce and Palouse Indians; they traded horses to the Crow and Blackfeet in the Black Hills.

The Boise Shoshoni were one of the first northern tribes to get horses from the Comanche Indians. Soon, horses grazed on the green grasses of the Boise River bottoms, where drinking water was good. This bottom land along the river was called Cop-cop-pa-ala, meaning Cottonwood Feast Valley. The Boise River Shoshonis and Eastern Shoshoni Indians conducted Trade Centers, as did the Cheyenne, Crow, Mandan and Nez Perce' tribes. The Boise Shoshoni Trade fair was held annually on the Snake River.

Comanche Indians were also credited with supplying horses to other tribes such as the Cayuse and Walla-Walla Indians. The Nez Perce and Palouse Indians received the Appaloosa horse from the Comanches; it became their favorite breed. The names Palouse Indian and Appaloosa are linked.

A trade route extended north to the Hidatsa, Mandan and Sioux, who first called horses "medicine dogs." These trade routes crisscrossed the northwest; horses reached the northwestern Indians by diffusion. Horses were also traded east to the Ponca and other tribes. Ponca Indian legend told of their tribe having received horses in trade from the Comanche Indians. They dwelled along the Niobrara River in now, Nebraska.

The Spanish Mustang was a sturdy buffalo and war horse for the Indians. The mustang was a small horse, about 15 hand-spans tall; it was golden brown with a black mane and tail.

Comanche buffalo hunters followed the bison onto the Southern Plains and were considered the very best buffalo hunters of the Plains Indians. Horse-mounted Comanches trekked for miles in order to reach the buffalo and follow them onto the Plains. Using their best buffalo horses, the Comanche warriors were well equipped for the hunt and avid horsemen.

They sent out scouts ahead to locate the buffalo herds, who reported back to them where he herd could be found. Hunting on horseback was an advantage in order to ride up within close proximity of the beasts. While riding at a gallop along-side the stampeding buffalo, an arrow, shot between the bison's ribs penetrated the lung and dropped the beast. The rifle was later used to hunt bison. A couple of clean shots from a rifle downed a buffalo.

Sometimes the lance was used to take down the buffalo. The buffalo lance was a hand-held 14 foot long spear used to thrust and jab or could

#31. Wild Mustangs in the Desert
Author Photo

#32. Warrior, Horse & Lance
Courtesy Azusa Publishing Company, LLC

be thrown. It was a very effective tool in hunting bison. The hunter rode alongside the buffalo, and with a few quick jabs of his lance could bring the animal down. The buffalo lance proved effective with the Indian, horse and buffalo. A vital spot on the buffalo was just behind the shoulder or the last rib. Buffalo was at the top of the food chain. Several braves rode together in a hunting party and garnered much meat.

A common hunting method of the Comanche was the buffalo surround. They formed a large circle around a small herd of wild buffalo and the hunters advanced, closing the circle, firing arrows into the buffalo.

The horse gave mobility to Plains Indian and introduced the travois, teepee and a new way of fighting. The Comanche made peace with the Ute Indians and conducted trade in Taos, New Mexico and were seen on the headwaters of the Arkansas River in 1700 and again in New Mexico in 1705.

Later, the Blackfeet traded with the Hudson's Bay Company for horses and firearms in 1730 and retaliated against the Shoshoni. The Blackfeet and their Assiniboine and Cree allies attacked a Shoshoni war party, killing many. The Blackfeet traded for horses from the Comanche Indians in 1754. In 1760, the Crow tribe also bartered horses from the Comanche people.

With the horse, guns and superior means of warfare, the powerful militant Blackfeet foe had a highly organized army and pushed the Shoshoni people and other tribes off the Plains, back into the mountains of Idaho. After that they continued on the war trail, raiding at night to take Shoshoni horses.

Legend tells us that Blackfeet war parties rode south for hundreds of miles, reaching the Spanish colonies in what became New Mexico Territory for horses. They stole hundreds of Spanish horses. They were gone over a two year period, before arriving in Blackfeet Country, trailing stolen horses. It was not long before they had built up good sized herds.

Comanche children were gifted ponies and learned to ride early. Boys and girls spent hours racing their ponies on an oval track or straightaway. Men, women and children were skilled in riding horses. Couples rode in the moonlight and over the sunny meadows together.

Young braves learned tricks on horseback, like leaning down picking up a bandanna on the ground while in the saddle. Their horses were agile and a brave could lean down and swing a comrade up onto his horse behind him in battle. Warriors made a loop that slipped over the horse's head. A brave leaned over beneath its head and could shoot or dodge arrows in battle at a full gallop. Comanche braves delighted in riding after Ute horsemen who were hunting buffalo on the plains and scared them off and scattering their camps.

The Comanche were horse husbandmen, like the Nez Perce. They literally loved their horses and sang songs to them, bathed them, braided their manes and tied ribbons in tails. Comanche Indians groomed and curried their horses and painted them with hand prints and other designs. Braves' bodies were fully painted to cause fear in the enemy in full regalia, armed with an array of war shields, guns, and lances 14 foot in length.

Comanche braves loved to go on raids and raided only at night to steal horses and count coup. They needed some visibility and a moon-lit night was desirable. This is how the term "Comanche moon" evolved.

If a Comanche warrior died, his horses were all killed and buried with him to ride in the afterlife. He was placed in the grave with his head toward the setting sun. The horses were buried, with their heads in the same direction. His bow and arrows, lance, scalp knife and tomahawk

#33. Appaloosa Horse
Courtesy Jumper/Sport

#34. "Appaloosa Colt"
Courtesy Jumper/Sport

were buried with him. The Comanche Shoshoni Indians believed the afterlife followed death and paralleled life on earth. They needed their horses to ride in Nirvana. When a Comanche woman passed away, her body was interred with the head toward the setting sun. The dead woman's calico dress, cooking kettle, fleshing knife and hide working tools and other belongings were buried next to her.

The Comanche Indians built up a surplus of horses and used them in trade to other tribes and to American and French fur traders. In 1723, Paducah Comanche traded horses and buffalo robes to a French trader, named Bourgmont in Kansas. The French traders came down the Mississippi from Canada, early and traded beads, blankets, guns, pots and metal arrowheads to the Comanche Indian tribe for buffalo hides and jerky.

The Comanche were an offshoot of the Northern Shoshoni people, who had trekked a great distance to discover a homeland of their own and were willing to fight for it.

The horse allowed the American Indian the freedom of movement to travel a great distance to hunt buffalo and changed their way of warfare. The horse and buffalo period was very fruitful for the Plains Indians.

The horse-mounted Indians hunted buffalo with ease from horseback. It provided their mode of transportation, hauled their goods and provided many a good horse race. At times the Comanche people ate horse meat. Horse riding in general was a popular sport.

The fierce Comanche warriors had become horse-mounted, dominating the Southern Plains and could not be defeated by other Indian tribes, the Spanish Army, Mexican Army, Texas Rangers and the U.S. Army. Comanches were fierce warrior horsemen "Lords of the Southern Plains."

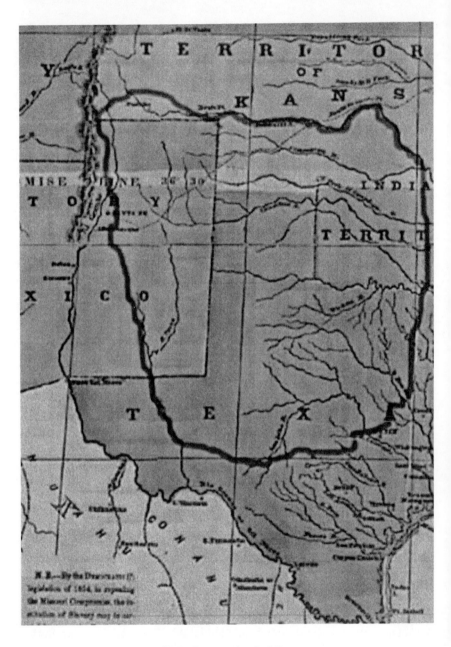

#35. Comancheria Map
Courtesy Footnote.com

Chapter Five
Comancheria

The Comanche Indians carved out a niche on the plains and came to dwell in their newly acquired territory. It covered Colorado, Kansas, New Mexico, Oklahoma and Texas. Comancheria is Spanish and most likely first came from the Mexican traders that bartered with these Indians. Comancheria means "the land of the Comanche," where they settled around the headwaters of the Brazos, Cimarron, Canadian and Red Rivers.

They ranged over the wooded areas, along streams, near the grassy plains that supported antelope, buffalo, deer and elk, as well as their horses and major waterways. Some streams were contaminated by animal carcasses and the water could not be drunk. The Comanche people located the fauna and flora needed to support them.

The Comanche Indians defended Comancheria against intruders on the High Plains south of the Arkansas River like a dynasty. Expert horsemen and fierce competitors, they were truly Lords of the Plains. They defeated most all enemy challengers and blocked the development for settling the Southern Plains by Spain, Mexico and Texans for over 150 years.

Buffalo, deer, eagle, horse and the mountain lion were sacred to them and animals made a major difference in the lives of the Plains Indians. Deerskin made clothing, like war shirts. Eagle feathers made beautiful war bonnets. The horse totally changed their movements and war. The mountain lion skins was revered and used for coverings. The Comanche ate a lot of buffalo, antelope, bear, deer, elk, moose and little or no fish.

The Comanche people preferred riverine encampments with close access to drinking water, water for cooking and to bathe in, especially winter camps in protected river valleys. The Indians built a wall around a natural hot springs with boughs for a roof. Steam-baths were used by the men to communally bathe as a social function and a meeting place. They could meet and socialize in the sweat lodge. After the sweat bath the men plunged into a cold river or stream.

Mineral hot springs used by the American Indians produced healing. Natural spring water was healthy for the body. More than just a bath or spa, the Indians used the hot springs for sacred ritual and were in tune with nature for healing the body. Hot water and nature's minerals were big medicine.

The Plains Comanche Indian relied on his gods and spiritual powers to guide him in life; being supernatural in nature led him down this path. The medicine man was the spiritual leader and advisor who used powerful magic.

The sacred pipe (calumet) was a ceremonial object to the Indians. The Indians smoked the pipe for treaties and for social reasons. The sacred pipe was smoked during fasting and prayer. The pipe was included in the sacred medicine bag. It was smoked in times of peace and before going on the war path. The pipe was smoked to form a bond of friendship or just for enjoyment. Pipes were fashioned from bone, clay, stone and wood. Figures of animals, birds or reptiles were carved on the pipes by certain members.

Decisions of the tribe on war, alliances, the hunt and camp moves were made in council, decided around the council fire, when they smoked the ceremonial pipe. Decisions were made according to custom passed down about important matters and from the elder's wisdom. The experienced, old and wise spoke in the council, while the young restless braves were silent. Disputes were solved by a wise chief. Many speeches and oratories were made with deliberation. Women were not heard, unless called to testify.

The peace chief presided in peaceable times and the war chief led them into battle in times of war. The hunt leader led the braves on the hunt. They practiced a very simple form of government by consent more than law. The tribal council controlled the vast territory and made sure that the people had ample food and was well protected. The Comanche army literally dominated their territory and did battle to keep their land and its buffalo herds.

The socio-political organization of the Comanche Indians was a true democratic process, having organized bands and band chiefs. The people voted to elect a band chief, who was to do their bidding. A band chief was chosen because of his experience on the hunt and his valor in war by the people (Newe). The band met in the council to discuss tribal matters. Dozens of bands formed and were scattered all around Comancheria. At one time there were thirty five bands in the Comanche Nation.

When a young man desired a wife, he went before the band council and told of his wishes. If the maiden or her parents had no objections, the council decided that they could live together for one moon. If all went well during that time, a period of another moon was extended. Again, if all continued well, they were formally married.

The Comanche populations were constantly shifting as the Indians moved around. The Indian population was broken down into a number of family lodges. Wealth was measured in horses owned, by counting coup and scalps taken. A feather was added to make a complete war bonnet for deeds of bravery fitting a war-chief. War bonnets or buffalo horn skull-caps were also worn during combat.

This Comanche tribe fought other tribes if it was eminent and the bold Comanche warriors fought every enemy tribe they faced. They literally fought everyone, including the Apache, Arapaho, Cheyenne,

Kiowa, Osage, Pawnee and the Ute Indian tribes and won their battles nearly every time.

They fought to maintain an empire and dominated the Southern Plains. They ranked in ferocity with the Blackfeet and Sioux Indian tribes of the Central Plains. Comanche warriors could handle the bow and arrow, rifle, spear and tomahawk on horseback like professional soldiers. They were expert horsemen and warriors, victorious in battle.

At the turn of the Eighteenth century, Spain recorded the Comanche Wars in America. The Spanish Army sent out patrols to engage them, but sometimes the patrols became disoriented in Comancheria and the Comanches simply ran off their horses and left the Spanish soldiers for dead.

Often the Spanish soldiers killed any small bands of Indians that they encountered, not knowing what tribe they were from, and just shot them because they were Indians.

Spain sent troops to investigate French trade but, they were massacred by Pawnee Indians, in 1720. The Comanches warred with the Plains Apache and Ute Indians and a year later, they fought the Nine-Days-War with the Apaches and dealt a major defeat to them at the Battle of the Mountain of Iron. Spanish troops were sent to aid the Apaches, but they did not locate them and sent an envoy to locate the Comanche Indians, but they had vanished.

Etienne Veniard de Bourgmont located the Comanche tribe on the upper Kansas River and also between the headwaters of the Kansas and the Platte Rivers, in Pawnee Indian Country in 1724.

Comanche Indians controlled the region of northeastern New Mexico, central Texas, and the Texas panhandle. The Comanche-Ute alliance failed around 1730. In 1745, the fifty year war with the Ute Indians began; the Comanche horsemen drove the Ute people into the mountains.

#36. "Wichita Indian Grass Hut"
Courtesy Western History Collections, University of Oklahoma Libraries

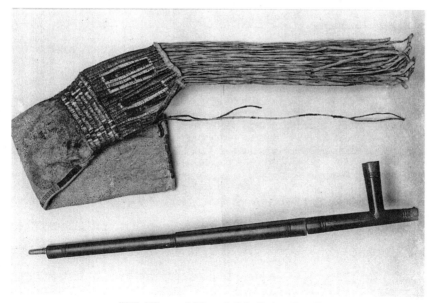

#37. "Sacred Pipe & Medicine Bag"
Courtesy Idaho State Historical Society

The *Kotsoteka* Comanche Indians crossed the Arkansas River into Mexico in 1745 and in 1746 the Comanche tribe went to war with the Spanish and attacked Pecos on New Mexico soil.

The widespread Comanche dialect over time became a common trade language of the Southwest, just as Chinook or Pigeon was spoken in the Northwest and Mobile in the Southeast. The Comanche language was spoken between various tribes in the Southwest along with universal sign language.

The French bartered peace between the Comanche and Wichita in 1747. The Wichita Indians were of the Caddoan language family, related linguistically to the Pawnee Indians.

In 1748, the Comanche tribe was admitted to the Taos New Mexico Trade Fair. The tribe was rich with plenty of wealth in horses to trade.

Lipan Apaches petitioned the Spanish to build a mission on the Comanche's land to cause a war between the Comanche people and the Spanish in 1749. The same year, the Comanche again broke an alliance with the Ute Indians. The French bartered a peace between the Comanche and the Wichita Indians. The Ute Indians begged the Spanish government to protect them from the fierce Comanche warriors.

The Spanish, on the other hand, spent much of their time seeking gold and silver. Spanish priests came to Christianize the Indians. The Comanche Indians traded with the French and Spanish, but preferred trading with the trusted French, who bartered with them for guns, but he Spanish did not provide them with guns. Spanish traders were reluctant to trade firearms to the Comanche warriors, knowing that they also attacked the Spanish.

In 1750, The Wichita Indians bartered peace between the Comanche, Osage and Pawnee Indians. That year, the Ute and Jicarilla Apache formed an alliance against the Comanche Indians.

The Comanches drove the Plains Apaches off of the Plains in 1750. The next year, the Comanche Indians defeated the Pawnee and drove them from the plains, into the Platte Valley region of what is now, Nebraska.

The Comanche traded horses to the French for firearms and moved into the Llano Estacado or Staked Plains of the Texas Panhandle. It seems that there were so few landmarks in that region, that wooden stakes had been used to mark the trail.

1757, the Lipan Apaches requested that a mission be established on Comanche land, which caused war between the Comanche Indians and Spain.

In 1758, Comanche and Wichita Indian warriors massacred San Saba Presidio village and the mission there, killing all. The Spanish Army was defeated at Red River by the combined forces of the Comanche and Wichita warriors in 1759. The Comanche Indians descended on the village of Taos, New Mexico in 1760 and 1761 and attacked the Lipan Apache mission on the Nueces River.

The British defeated the French, ending the French & Indian War. On February 10, 1763, the Treaty of Paris was signed. France ceded Louisiana Territory to Spain. The French left America and the French fur traders also departed. The Indians lost some good trading partners.

In 1768, the Ute and Jicarilla Apaches were defeated by Comanche braves. In 1771, the town of Laredo emerged. Comanche Indians drove the occupants from the north bank of the Rio Grande River. They reconstructed and re-named the town, Nuevo Laredo on the south side of the Rio Grande.

The northern Mexican province depended on farming and ranching. Comanche Indians were a definite threat to Spanish American colonists.

A Spanish military post was built in San Antonio, housing eight companies of soldiers. There were large camps of winter villages northwest of San Antonio. In 1774, Spanish soldiers, joined by Pueblo Indians, attacked a Comanche village near Raton and took 100 prisoners.

The Comanche Indians fought all intruders on their soil. First they fought the Spanish Army and then the Mexicans. In 1774, Spanish colonists established a village, called Pueblo de Bucareli, in Comanche territory that lasted until 1778, when a Comanche war party attacked them. Comanche braves took 200 horses and destroyed the village. The Spanish colonists killed only three Comanche warriors.

The Kiowa Indians' ancestors migrated from Canada into Montana and the Yellowstone region before moving into the Black Hills. It is told that the Kiowa bartered for the horse from the Crow Indians. In 1775, the strong Lakota Sioux Indians drove the Kiowa out of the Black Hills onto the Plains.

The Yamparika Comanche Army fought the Sioux and Cheyenne Warriors in the Black Hills in 1775. In 1777, New Spain held a war council, incorporating allies from the northern Indian tribes for a peaceful alliance with the Comanche and Wichita Indians. Peace was made between most Comanche chiefs, but they could not control the actions of the young reckless braves on the war path. Comanches shared their territory with the Wichitas.

In the year 1779, the Comanche had talks of peace, but 500 Spanish soldiers, combined with 259 Apache and Ute Indian scouts, under, Don Juan Bautista De Anza, assaulted a Comanche village deep in Comanche country on the eastern Colorado plateau. Governor de Anza and 500 soldiers attacked and massacred women and children in Chief Green Horn's village on their turf and destroyed their lodges, while the chief and his warriors were absent on the war trail. The Spanish captured 500 of the Comanche's horses.

De Anza rode to the south side of the Arkansas River and lay in ambush for the chief and his returning war party. De Anza and his horse-mounted lancers lay in wait for their arrival. When the Chief and his warriors returned, de Anza and the Spanish Army massacred them all. He wanted to teach them a lesson by giving them a dose of their own medicine.

The Comanche retaliated with even greater ferocity seeking revenge. The Indian uprising was out of control by 1780. Domingo Cabello, governor of Texas, was complained to of daily Comanche raids on ranches. He did not have enough soldiers to protect the ranchers, nor did they know the location of the next raid. The fierce Comanche braves literally dominated Comancheria. Spanish troops were beaten every time they fought them in their own territory.

De Anza gave the Comanche Indians blankets contaminated with smallpox that took its toll. The Comanche and Wichita Indians were devastated by the smallpox that Anza's soldiers had given them. The plague killed many Comanche Indians, in 1780.

The Spanish Army surprised isolated bands of Comanche Indians and killed them. De Anza purposefully sent captives back to their bands with a message. When you are ready for peace; we will cooperate. Briefly, time, the Spanish had the upper-hand in defeating the northern Comanche Indians.

Subsequently, several Comanche chiefs came to Anza wanting peace. They deliberated and the Comanche and the Spanish Army bartered a peace between them. A treaty signed with one Comanche band was not honored by other bands, so Anza insisted on just one Comanche chief to represent them. Chief Leather Jacket was chosen.

#38. Comanche Camp
Courtesy Legends of America.com

#39. "Ute Warrior & Bride"
Courtesy Azusa Publishing Company, LLC

They retreated southward and entered Comanche Indian territory. In 1780, the Kiowa and Comanche Indians clashed on their northern border at the Arkansas River, but later withdrew to the south side of the Arkansas.

In 1781, America was born, having received their independence from England. The British surrendered to General George Washington on October 19, 1781 at Yorktown; the victory ended the Revolution.

In 1785, the Spanish signed a treaty with the Texas Comanche chiefs. The Comanche warriors raided Pecos again and again and would later raid Taos. The braves went on the war trail with New Spain.

In July of 1785, after the Greenhorn Massacre, Comanche warriors came in under a flag of truce. De Anza had beaten them at their own game. He refused to talk peace until all of the Comanche were represented. That year De Anza called a great council in Taos. The Comanche Indians assembled, represented by Chief Cuera (Leather Jacket), who was elected by the people.

Comanche Chief Toro Blanco, known as White Bull opposed the choice of Chief Cuera to represent them.. There was an altercation and Chief White Bull was slain for resisting the treaty signing, in 1786. The Spanish Army, also bartered peace between the Comanche and Ute tribes. The Spanish presented a treaty to the Comanche and Ute tribes that they signed.

By then De Anza had won the respect of the Comanche people. He did not make demands of them. He simply offered a peace agreement, with a chance to trade with the Spanish or war. At this time the Spanish Army began to reward peaceable chiefs with medals, much the same as the U.S. Army. Chief Cuera was honored with a ceremony and was given a saber and a banner and other gifts such as insignias, medals, titles and uniforms.

The Comanches promised no more war in New Mexico and De Anza cleverly included the Ute Indians. The truce with the Comanche and Ute Indians relaxed tensions between them. Now, the Comanche entered a town to trade horses, while Mexican traders moved freely on the frontier plains.

Part of the peace with the Comanche and Ute Indians was the agreement to join with the Spanish and fight the western Apache Indians. The Comanche partnered with the Ute Indians to raid deep into Mexico in pursuit of horses to terrorize the Mexicans. The truce between the Comanche Indians and Ute Indians was eventually broken, but held in New Mexico.

The Spanish aided the Comanche braves in war. A combined force of Spanish soldiers and Comanche warriors rallied in 1789, to defeat the Lipan Apache Nation. The Spanish also aided the Comanche Indians by giving them food in famine. The Comanche retaliated by allowing the Spanish safe passage through their country. The Comanche and Spanish worked well together.

Apaches continued to raid in Texas Territory and Mexico, targeting small Comanche encampments, taking plunder and captives. Missions and villages were left in ruin. Comanche and the Spanish army attacked an Apache-Ute village, north of Santa Fe and prisoners were sold into slavery.

Spanish soldiers rode deep into the interior only to discover their vacant campground. Comanche marauders first raided New Mexico for horses while, Ute Indians conducted trade in villages in New Mexico.

Comanche warriors attacked an Osage Indian village and massacred them, in 1791 near the Kansas-Missouri border.

The Comanche tribe was divided over one dozen semi-autonomous bands. Like the Shoshoni, they were named for the seasonal food group they ate at the time, for example. Pena (honey) and teka (eaters) were called the Penateka band (Honey eaters) or the Wasps. Kotso (buffalo) and teka (eaters) were called Kotsoteka or (Buffalo eaters) and the Yamparikas were called Root eaters. Many bands were formed and the number of Comanche Indians grew to around 20,000 strong in the mid 1800s with five major bands: the Kotsoteka, Kwaharu, Nayukas, Penatekas and Yamparikas.

Ceremonial dances were a sign of victory. The Comanche did the Buffalo Dance, Eagle Dance, Ghost Dance, Green Corn Dance, Horse Dance, Scalp Dance, Vengeance Dance, Victory Dance and the War Dance.

The headdress was a symbol of power. Otter skin caps were symbolic and worn during raids. Buffalo-horn war-bonnets were symbols of their might (power). Bravery in battle and war feats showed their magic and signs of strength.

The Smoke signal was a method used by the Comanche Indians to send messages to other members of their band up to 50 miles away. A camp fire was lit on a high butte and green grass was placed on the fire, to produce a dense, white smoke. A blanket was then spread over the smoldering fire and released to send puffs of smoke into the air. The smoke signal was seen a long distance away and the code was deciphered by the other Comanche Indians.

When the Comanche war parties went on the war trail, they left spare horses tethered nearby. That way, they had fresh mounts for a hasty retreat and took pack mules along on buffalo hunting excursions to transport the buffalo meat and robes.

The Comanche Indians enjoyed stealing horses from enemy tribes and counting coup. They seemed to believe that these tribes should share their horses with them.

There is an old Comanche legend told of a young brave, who asked his father's permission to go along with a war party. His father told him, alright, take this pony and lead it from a mule. When you reach enemy territory, ride the pony fast and then stop. Do this four times and he will never tire. The story went on to explain that the young brave went on to be successful in battle and was honored for his actions. Members of the tribe did not smoke the pipe before him out of respect.

Hawakakeno (Wide River) was a mighty Comanche warrior. He was a great warrior on the war trail and the most renown in his village. Everyone in his band looked up to him.

Many Europeans had arrived in North America east of the Mississippi. Settlers and other various foreign Indian tribes from the east began to trespass on Comanche lands. After 1800, the western frontier remained a wilderness, inhabited mostly by Indians and wild animals.

President Thomas Jefferson became President in 1801 and sent a secret message to Congress urging that trade be established with the Indians. He urged them to raise livestock, grow crops and enter into manufacturing.

In 1803, the president signed the Louisiana Purchase with France for $15,000,000.000, doubling the size of America and adding the territory west of the Mississippi to the Rocky Mountains, between Canada and Mexico.

Jefferson was interested in the land west of the Rockies to the Pacific Ocean and wanted an expeditionary team to explore it. He asked Congress for monies for the mission; Congress responded with only $2500 to bankroll the trip. President Thomas Jefferson authorized the military expedition of Captain Meriwether Lewis and Captain William Clark in 1803 to lead an expedition of the Corp of Discovery with 31 army corps

#40.
Jicarilla Apache Chief
Courtesy Azusa Publishing
Company, LLC

#41. "Kachina Apache Dancers"
Courtesy Azusa Publishing Company, LLC

and hired men cross-country to the Pacific Ocean, opening up a whole new hemisphere for western expansion.

The Corp journeyed from St. Louis to the upper Missouri River Valley region of what is now North Dakota. Lewis and Clark reached the Sioux speaking Mandan Village on the north bank of the Missouri River and were greeted by Toussaint Charbonneau, a French-Indian fur trapper. They hired Charbonneau as interpreter and met his wife, Sacajawea (Bird Woman). The expedition successfully reached the Pacific in 1804 and returned the next year.

Early American and French fur traders and the explorers knew the Comanche Indians they contacted as the "Padoucah Indians," their Siouan name. Lewis and Clark wrote in their journals about having seen the tribe, known as the Padoucah Indians, hunting for buffalo along the Upper Missouri.

The Hudson's Bay Company, French and American fur companies traded for countless furs and buffalo hides; as a result, buffalo populations diminished to a great extent.

After a Kiowa man spent the summer among the Comanche, the two tribes made peace in 1805. In 1807, Dr. John Sibley met with a Comanche chief. The Kiowa Apache Indians signed a peace treaty with the Army about 1810.

In 1811, the Comanche Chief Sordo visited Bexar and was imprisoned in Coahuila, which incited the Comanche Indians to break relations with Texas. In 1813, American traders bartered with them for horses and in 1816, trader John Jamison, also traded with the Comanche people.

Andrew Jackson was a proponent of Indian Removal and led the military to defeat the Creek Indians in 1813-1814; the Indians forfeited 22 million acres of land in Alabama and Georgia.

The white men brought cholera and smallpox and hundreds of Comanche Indians succumbed to the deadly diseases. The Indians were appalled at the amount of white men that had trespassed on their land. The Comanche war parties rode into Mexico and contracted cholera, smallpox and venereal diseases. They had terrible losses from smallpox in 1818.

The U.S. Army attacked the Seminole Indians for harboring Negro fugitives and refusing to sell lands to the government. The Seminole Wars were fought in 1817-1818. The Seminoles lost and Jackson negotiated nine peace treaties out of ten in the east.

In 1821, the Santa Fe Trail was opened. Spanish rule was replaced by Mexico in 1821. The Mexican government ruled in the Southwest for the next 15 years. Mexico made a treaty with the Texas Comanche Indians a year later; shortly thereafter, Mexico broke the treaty and the Rio Grande War erupted in 1825. That year, the Comanche Indians raided Chihuahua. Mexico and the Comanche Indians signed another treaty in 1826. In 1829, the Comanche and Kiowa Indians fought the U.S. Army in combat on the Santa Fe Trail.

Newspaper journalists covering the Indian Wars often contributed to bad sentiment among the gentry against the Indians because of their raids and killing white settlers, deciding that the Indians were all bad.

Like an eye-for-an-eye, the Comanche warriors demanded that the exact number of white people die to avenge a friend or family member's deaths, who had been killed by the white man's army or the white men. In one odd case, the mother of a white family was killed while the father and children were spared.

The Comanche Indians resented Texans and did not understand their role in America. They hated the white intruders on their lands. The enmity grew and their war parties constantly attacked white settlements.

The U.S. Army retaliated with a raid on an encampment or larger village of Comanche Indians killing women and children. In turn, a Comanche war party would seek revenge by massacring a white settlement. Enmity grew between them in a vicious circle. The Army used every means of defeating the Indians: ambush, disease massacre, killing off the buffalo, reduction of land, warfare etcetera.

The Cherokee Indians wrote their own language and in 1827; they created their own constitution, modeled after that of the U.S. In 1828-35, they published a newspaper, called the Phoenix, in Cherokee and English.

The Indian Removal Act was signed into law May 28, 1830, by President Jackson. The act authorized him to grant unsettled lands west of the Mississippi River for Indian lands within eastern state borders. Some tribes went peaceably; others resisted.

Indian Nations were declared sovereign in order to be able to cede land, based on Georgia law of 1830, which prohibited white settlers from trespassing on Indian lands. The American Indians could occupy land, but not hold title to it.

The Indians east of the Mississippi River were conquered by the U.S. Army and forced to relinquish millions of acres of land to the United States government and were pushed off their land. White settlers had pressured the government to acquire Indian lands for planting crops and building their homes. The Indians were displaced to west of the Mississippi River in Indian Territory.

George Catlin, famous artist who wrote about the Indians, estimated the Comanche's numbers to be 30-40,000 in 1830. They had endless resources from millions of buffalo and tens of thousands of antelope and wild horses.

The Georgia Supreme court, in 1831, declared that Cherokee Indians had the right to self government, but Jackson refused to enforce it. He regarded the Indians as children, who needed guidance and believed that the Indian Removal Act would protect the Indians and allow them to govern themselves in peace. Missionaries that aided in resisting removal were lawfully removed, themselves. Some of the citizenry protested against Indian removal and said that it was a brutal and inhumane treatment of the Indians.

Mexico banned trade with Comanche tribe in 1831. In 1832, the Comanche caught enemy Pawnee Indians stealing horses and killed all of the Pawnee. In 1834, Mexico renegotiated peace with the Texas Comanche Indians; then the same year dishonored the settlement and the Comanche warriors resumed their raids on the Mexicans.

In 1834, a region of Oklahoma was established as "Indian Territory." A former possession of the United States in eastern Oklahoma, Indian Territory covered 31,000 square miles.

Natives of that region were in disagreement about giving up land to the eastern intruders, the Comanche Indians, in particular. Eastern tribes settled on Comanche hunting grounds and they went to war.

As part as the Jefferson Plan, all Indian peoples were to be relocated from the eastern United States to Indian Territory. These Indians were told that region would be theirs. The government moved the eastern tribes into Comancheria in Indian Territory in Oklahoma and they were given better provisions than the Plains Indians, who resented the intrusion.

The Five Civilized Tribes were hesitant to take possession of assigned lands, due to Comanche raiding parties. The Creek, Cherokee, Chickasaw, Delaware, and Seminole Indian tribes were honored by being called, "the Five Civilized Tribes." Most of these had slaves and were

77

#42.
Trail of Tears Trail Marker
Courtesy Footnote.com

#43.
Ute Woman,
Child & Cradleboard
Courtesy Azusa Publishing
Company, LLC

forced to free them after the Civil War. These eastern tribes were given land west of the Mississippi River. As the foreign Indian tribes moved in from the east, as well as settlers onto their lands. The government took Comanche lands in exchange for the reservation.

Their total population was 884,507 people and they were given 19,475,614 acres at the time, averaging 230 acres for every man, woman and child. They resisted by holding onto their land from sale to the government. They adopted large-scale farming, to comply with government demands.

There was much corruption in the government. Finally a new Indian Commission was formed. The Indian Commission had joint jurisdiction with the Department of the Interior over Indian affairs and appropriations.

President Grant wanted to instate the Indian Commission under the U.S. Army. Comanche Indians were a proud race, bold and daring. The socio-political structure of the Comanche warriors was a military one. The horse-mounted Comanche army was nearly unbeatable.

In 1834, the U.S. government stepped in to stop the war and negotiated a peace between the Comanche Indians and the eastern tribes. The Comanches signed, but not willingly, because of others living on the outskirts of their territory; yet they respected the agreement.

Other Americans began moving into Comanche Territory at the same time settlers forged across Comancheria on their way west to Oregon and California and, however, the Comanche warriors did not welcome strangers.

The towns of Sonora, Chihuahua and Durango, Mexico established bounties for Comanche scalps. The Comanche Tribe signed a treaty with the American government in 1835, but continued to raid other tribes for horses.

In the autumn of 1838-39, the U.S. government made the Cherokee Indians trek on a forced march cross country over The "Trail of Tears" to Indian Territory in Oklahoma; 4,000 Cherokees died on the long journey.

In 1840, a peace treaty was bartered between the Comanche, Kiowa and Kiowa-Apache Indians and with the Cheyenne and Arapaho tribes.

In 1845, the Republic of Texas became a state and was backed by the federal government. The Comanche Indians became an even more powerful adversary; as over 70,000 Americans rushed into Texas.

Thousands of miners moved across the Comanche territory, during the California Gold Rush in 1848. In the Gold Rush of 1849, the Asiatic cholera was introduced to the Southern Plains. The Comanche and Kiowa Indians lost over half of their populations because of the white man's diseases.

Much of Comancheria had been settled by Euro-Americans by 1855. First, the French Traders came and then the Spanish Traders arrived. Spanish and Mexican soldiers came from the south. Texas vigilantes and Texas Rangers fought them, followed by the U.S. Army.

The Comanche Indians fought to gain territory for their tribe and were not about to let go of it. The Comanche warriors fought any intruders that encroached on Comancheria. The Spanish and Mexican governments, settlers, the Texas Rangers and the U.S. Army all fought them.

It was opened up as Indian Territory and the Eastern Tribes arrived. They were fighting a losing battle. The Comanche tribe would live to see the size of their reservation shrink.

Chapter Six
Comancheros

The Comanches were horse brokers, equestrian Indians who owned a large number of horses and maintained wealth from these large herds. They stole thousands of horses and built up hundreds of stock. The Comanche traded with the French traders and were no strangers to barter. They also took part in trafficking of slaves that they had captured. The Comanche language became a trade language with the other tribes in the southwest.

Early on, Comanche Indians traded at trade fairs in Taos and the Pueblos and did some trading in Santa Fe and other Spanish villas. The Comanche traders bartered buffalo hides and horses to the reservation.

They also conducted trade fairs. Trade fairs were accompanied by festive celebrations. The pipe was smoked; there was song, dance and storytelling by both genders. Gambling and horse racing were a favorite pastime. Comanches traded buffalo robes, horses, bow and arrows, knives and wives.

Spanish Governor, Juan Baptiste de Anza signed a treaty of 1786 with the Indians of the Plains allowing trade between New Mexico and the Indians. In return, the Comanches were to be peaceable toward the Spaniards in Texas. This was the beginning of the long association between the Comanche Indians and the Mexican traders.

New Mexico was a trade Mecca and Santa Fe was its center. Anza' peace agreement allowed freedom of movement and free trade. This gave the Mexican traders freedom to travel in Comancheria. Mexican merchants moved freely back and forth across the Mexican border in order to trade goods, chiefly with the Comanche Indians for over 100 years. The

Spanish Army named them, "Comancheros." The U.S. Army also picked up the term. People assumed that they had Comanche blood, which was a misnomer.

Comancheros were actually half-breed Mexican traders, natives of north-central New Mexico and the western Texas frontier who traded with the Southern Plains Indians in their own territory. New Mexico at that time was made up mainly of "gringos," Indians, mixed Spanish and Indian blood and Spanish. Comancheros were trusted Hispanic traders, who bartered with them and were allowed safe-passage to enter into their territory. They were the counter-part of the fur traders of the Northwest. They banded together and ventured into frontier country to trade for horses and mules and also took a meager amount of beads, cloth, trinkets and other goods for trade.

The Comancheros ranged over a large area, from the Wichita Mountains of Oklahoma, southeast to the Davis Mountains in Texas and north to the Dakotas. Their center of trade was the region known as Llano Estacado and Palo Duro Canyon, both in Comanche Territory where there were also Kiowa and Comanche villages. Comancheros first brought their goods in by pack-mule and later hauled their goods by oxen drawn ox-carts (carteras) to the Indian villages. They followed old Indian trails that became deep ruts, after the Comanchero's wagons cut into the desert soil for decades.

The victory in battle paved the way for peace talks. In 1785, Governor de Anza and War-chief Ecueracapa, elected to represent the Comanche Nation, signed the peace treaty between the Comanche Indians and the Spanish Army. This opened up trade with them.

In 1790, a peace was made between the Comanche and Kiowa when the two tribes arrived at a Comanchero trading camp at the same time. The panicked Comanchero trader bartered a truce to save lives.

Comanche women scraped and tanned the buffalo hides and prepared the robes. They were traded to the Hispanic traders for trade goods, like guns, ammunition and other goods. They traded manufactured wares such as beads, blankets, cloth, hatchets, knives, pots and pans to the Comanche Indians. The Mexican traders bartered tobacco and whiskey to the Comanche Indians. Food stuffs, such as bread, coffee and flour were also traded to the Indians for buffalo hides and jerky. Metal trade points were also a Comanche favorite.

The Comanche waged war from Kansas to Texas and into New Mexico. Federal law prevented Indians' being arrested by soldiers or federal officers, unless on reservations with the agent's permission. They continued to fight the Ute Indians. They hunted the buffalo and traded buffalo hides to the Mexican traders for guns and ammunition who also provided the Comanche with the ten-shot lever action repeating rifles. The Comanche Indians had progressed from the bow and arrow to modern weaponry in a few short years.

In the 100 year history of trade with these Indians, the Comancheros entered into the illicit slave-trade with them. The Mexican traders, at times, ransomed slaves from the Comanches. At first, the Comancheros bartered only Indian captives for mine workers and servants. But in time, they accepted Mexican slaves in trade.

Sometimes, the traders held captives of noble birth for handsome rewards from relatives in northern Mexico, Texas and sometimes from American government officials. It was Mexican traders, who would ransom Rachael Parker Plummer from the Comanches and transport her to Santa Fe.

The Treaty of Laramie was signed on November 4, 1868, with the Plains Arapaho, Cheyenne, Crow and Sioux Indian tribes. The chiefs all met with Gen.William Tecumseh Sherman and peace commissioners to negotiate the most important treaty in the 19th Century. Chief Red Cloud attended. The treaty closed the Bozeman Trail and created the Great Sioux Reservation in the Black Hills.

Fetterman's Outpost, on the Bozeman Trail and Elliot's Squadron, on the Wichita were wiped out by Comanche attack in 1868. Frustrated, General Sherman ordered his officers to eradicate as many Indians as possible, to reduce their numbers.

During the Civil War, federal contractors furnished the Union Army with the meat to feed the soldiers. Arizonian and New Mexican cattle buyers had a market for thousands of beeves.

Quanah's band traded almost exclusively with the Comancheros and while the marauding Comanche raiders attacked frontier settlements on the Texas frontier; they drove off their livestock and bartered them to the Comancheros, who sold the cows to the Arizonian and New Mexican cattle buyers and ranchers, no questions asked.

The Comancheros had a new industry. They traded wagon loads of repeating rifles to the Comanche Indians for stolen cows. At the end of the war this practice stopped.

The War Between the States had stripped the forts of about 60,000 soldiers, who joined the confederate Army, leaving only 25,000 officers and enlisted men in 1869 for duty men to defend Texans on the frontier against Indians. The ragtag soldiers were undisciplined and half of those recruits deserted to avoid serving in the Indian Wars.

Immigrant wagon trains crossed Kansas and Colorado as the war ended by the hundreds and were being attacked on a regular basis by Comanche marauders, from the Arkansas River to the Rio Grande and along the Santa Fe Trail. They continued to raid Mexican settlements and neighboring tribes. In the north, Comanche Indians traded peacefully with white fur traders and Comancheros.

In 1869, the Comanches were free to roam off the reservation. There were no rules to restrict their movement. Two-thirds of the Comanche people arrived and resided on the reservation. The remaining third continued to go on the war path and hunt as they had been accustomed.

The Indians complained of the lack of firearms for hunting to provide enough food for their families, so the Department of the Interior delivered several tons of new-model repeating Spencer and Henry rifles to the Indians of the Southern Plains, although it was illegal under federal law to sell guns to the Indians., while the U.S. Army still carried older single-shot models.

They became better equipped than the U.S. Army, courtesy of the American government. Now, equipped with modern repeating rifles, they could hunt and raid to their heart's content which they did. The Comanche war-parties attacked settlers and gold miners that traveled across Comanche Territory.

Rumors of Mexican traders, dealing in rustled cattle and ransomed slaves was giving them a bad reputation. The squabble over stolen cattle became a problem and the U.S. Army finally had to intervene, which resulted in the eventual downfall of the Comanchero's trade pact with the Comanche Indians. The Mexican traders and the Comanche Indians had bonded and bartered together for over 100 years and now it was coming to an end. The Comanche Indians had finally lost their long-time New Mexican "Comanchero" traders, just as they had their favored French fur trading partners.

#44.
Kiowa Chief Lone Wolf
Courtesy Azusa Publishing
Company, LLC

#45.
Famous Kiowa Chief Satanta
Courtesy Azusa Publishing
Company, LLC

Chapter Seven
Kiowa Allies

The Kiowa Indians called themselves Naheeshandeenah, meaning "our kind." The Kiowa were horse riding, Plains Indians, who had been driven out of the Black Hills by the fierce Lakota Sioux Indian warriors in 1765. The nomadic Kiowa dwelled in the region of Texas and New Mexico known as the Texas panhandle, including western Oklahoma and eastern New Mexico.

The Kiowa and the Comanche Indians were very much alike; they were Plains Indians who hunted the buffalo. Their attire, lodges, hair style and buffalo culture highly resembled the Comanche Indians and were hunters and gatherers. Men hunted; women gathered berries, grasses, nuts and roots. Boys learned to hunt and tend the horses; the girls learned to do women's work from their mothers. Social groups were age graded.

The Kiowa spoke Tanoan (Kiowa-Tanoan), as did the Pueblo Indians in the Rio Grande River Valley. Tiwa and Tewa are Tanoan languages. Most Tanoan speakers lived in New Mexico along the Rio Grande River. The Tigua, near El Paso were Tanoan speakers. Tigua in Spanish is Tiwa and pronounced nearly the same.

The Taos Pueblo Indians in northern New Mexico spoke Tiwa, as did the Isleta Pueblo Indians. Pueblos in the Texas panhandle, abandoned in circa,1350-1400 may have been Kiowan. It is speculated that the Jumana Indians may have been predecessors of the Kiowa.

Kiowa Indians are noted for originating the sign language. They were the most prolific sign talkers on the Plains, along with the Teton Dakota (Sioux). It was very useful in that any Indian tribe using universal sign language could understand the member of a different tribe that spoke another dialect. Sign language was universal among most American Indian tribes. The American Indian sign language is still used today, primarily at ceremonies, festivals and intertribal powwows.

The Plains Kiowa Indians practiced the ritual of the Sun Dance. They formed a large ring of teepees for the Sun Dance and other festivities. The Kiowa Indians developed a strong warrior society. They were horse warriors and a buffalo society. The Kiowa tribe strongly resembled the Comanche Indian culture. Like the Comanches they always warred on horseback. Kiowas stole horses from the Spanish and earned the name, "the thieves."

In 1681, the explorer, La Salle met the Kiowa (Gallacka) tribe in Illinois, which was their name for themselves. Kiowa Indians are not to be confused with the Kiowa-Apache tribe, although they were bonded. The two tribes developed an affinity for one another, as close as blood brothers.

The Kiowas and Kiowa-Apaches lived close-by in the Black Hills in peace and harmony. They intermarried and became closely bonded. The name, Kiowa-Apache developed from that association. The Kiowa-Apache were an isolated group of Plains Apaches, not to be confused with the Apaches of the southwest.

An old Indian legend told of a Kiowa warrior who was captured by the Comanche. The band held council and the decision was to put him to death, but one Comanche head man disagreed and asked that he be freed, lest one day he might return the favor.

The council reversed the decision and the warrior was sent home with honor. He was given a horse, saddle and bridle and given his freedom. The warrior rode back to his camp where he described the Comanche's kindnesses. A treaty was signed with the Spanish Governor of New

#46.
"Sitting in the Saddle,"
son of Lone Wolf
Courtesy Azusa Publishing
Company, LLC

#47.
Kiowa Papoose
in Cradleboard
Courtesy Western
History Collections,
University of Oklahoma
Libraries

Mexico, Juan Bautista de Anza and the Comanche Indians, allowing trade between the New Mexico Indians and New Mexico in return for protection of Texas and against intruders on Spanish Territory in 1786.

In 1790, a truce and temporary peace was bartered between the Comanche and Kiowa Indians. That truce kept the peace and led to an alliance between the two tribes which would later make peace between them. In 1805, a formal peace was made between the Comanche and Kiowa Indians, who never forgot the Comanche act of kindness that would be the beginning of a long lasting friendship between them.

The Comanche Indians shared their lands with the Kiowa and Wichita allies. The Comanche and Kiowa Indians became close friends and soon intermarried and bonded; one tribe may have acted as the bride donor tribe to the other. The Kiowa Indians became the Comanche tribe's closest allies; they melded together and in a short time became inseparable. When the Comanche warriors raided, the Kiowa Indians often joined them on the war path.

The Kiowa and Comanche Indian tribes bonded together to hunt the buffalo and to go on the war trail. The Kiowas were noted for their long raids into Canada and Mexico, like the Comanche. The Kiowa and the Yamparika Comanche Indians signed the peace agreement, the Atkinson Treaty in 1853.

Stumbling or Charging Bear (Sa-tim-gear) was born in 1832 and became chief of the Kiowa Indians. He was the cousin of the great Kiowa Chief Kicking Bird. In 1854, Kiowa Chief Stumbling Bear led a war party against the Pawnee Indians, to avenge the death of his brother, but ran into an enemy band of Fox-Sauk warriors, who drove them off with smoke sticks (rifles and ammunition). The Kiowa were a lot like the Comanches and fought as their allies.

In 1856, Chief Stumbling Bear led a successful raid against the Navajo Indians, taking spoils from them. In the 1860's he led raids into the Texas frontier and allied with Chiefs Satanta and Satank were formidable foes. In 1865, Stumbling Bear's warriors fought Kit Carson and his forces.

Kicking Bird was born in 1835. He was wise and a strong Kiowa chief. His grand-father was a Crow Indian captive that the Kiowa adopted into their tribe. In Wichita, Kansas, the chief signed the Kiowa Treaty of 1865 that preceded the 1867 Treaty of Medicine Lodge.

In the Medicine Lodge Treaty of 1867, the Kiowa-Apache were reunited with the Kiowa tribe. The Arapaho, Cheyenne, Comanche, Kiowa and Plains Apache Indians signed the Medicine Lodge Treaty. Some famous chiefs that signed were Black Kettle, Brave Man, Satank, Satanta, Spotted Wolf and Ten Bears. Chief Quanah refused to sign.

Stumbling Bear and his cousin Kicking Bird promoted peace as acting "civil or peace chiefs." In 1872, Stumbling Bear joined the Kiowa delegation of chiefs to Washington D.C. and in 1878, the government built him a home on the Oklahoma reserve at Fort Sill, where he died in 1903. Chief Stumbling Bear was the last Kiowa chief from the Plains days to pass.

In 1891, the Kiowa-Apache's numbers were 325. That year, they suffered from a measles epidemic and in 1892, their population diminished to only 275 people and by 1905, just 155.

Chief Kicking Bird and his people did not war against the Americans or fight the move to the reservation, with little reward. White men encroached on reservation land and stole their cattle and horses, while buffalo hunters trespassed on Kiowa land to hunt and discouraged relations with the Kiowas. Kicking Bird fought for the first tribal school. The Chief died May 3, 1875.

#48. Kiowa Indian Princesses
Courtesy Western History Collections
University of Oklahoma Libraries

Satanta was born around 1840 and also became chief of the Kiowa Indians. He stood six feet tall and was very muscular and sat high in the saddle. He was an accomplished orator and had a sense of humor.

A humorous anecdote about Chief Satanta occurred on July of 1864. He led a band of Kiowa braves to take horses at Fort Learned, Kansas; the raid was a success, as the Indians took the whole herd. The next time that Satanta saw the Commander of the post, he told him that the horses they took were bad and that he should get some new ones.

In the autumn of 1864, Kit Carson led the New Mexico Volunteers against the Kiowa and Comanche Indians in New Mexico. During the fray the Volunteers had become confused by the repeated sound of bugle calls. In actuality, the horn was blown by Chief Satanta; he loved the bugle that he had captured as coup in another battle.

The Army attempted to win over the Indians at the peace table. Satanta was among several Kiowa chiefs at a peace council; he spoke to the other chiefs, saying he wanted no part of peace.

George Armstrong Custer was impressed with Satanta, and awarded him a military uniform. Later, Chief Satanta, wearing his new uniform and blowing his bugle, led an attack against Custer's B Company of 7th Cavalry and ran off all of their horses. The chief was not so impressive, then.

At the end of the Civil War, in 1865 there was unrest on the Southern Plains. The Comanche and Kiowa tribes made war on the citizens of Texas and New Mexico Territories. In the spring of 1871, Kiowa braves lay in ambush and attacked a Butterfield Stage line in western Texas.

The day before a raid, a Kiowa shaman envisioned an owl hooting. The medicine man interpreted the vision as two parties coming down a trail. The first party was to go free. They were to attack the second party to pass.

A Kiowa war party of 100 warriors watched as a small squadron of soldiers passed by; just hours later, the second party, a wagon train, proceeded by. The Kiowa war party ambushed the wagons; Satanta blew his bugle for attack. They killed seven teamsters. The first party to pass included General William Tecumsah Sherman, his life spared because of the shaman's vision.

Chief Satanta was prosecuted in Texas for the deaths of the team and found guilty. Satanta addressed the court, "If you will let me go to my people, I will withdraw my warriors from Texas. I will take them across the Red River and that shall be the line between us and the pale faces. I will wash out spots of blood and make it a white land and there shall be peace, and the Texans may plow and drive their oxen to the banks of the river."

The judge responded, "You shall be hung, hung, hung!" He was not impressed. Satanta vowed to fight no more; but the Texas Governor commuted his sentence to life imprisonment. He had been arrested by the Army, repeatedly. Satanta was paroled.

In 1874, while Chief Satanta was peacefully buffalo hunting, a Kiowa war party executed a raid, that he was wrongfully accused of leading. Rather than cause more grief to his people, Satanta surrendered. While in prison, in Huntsville, Texas, Satanta committed suicide on October 11, 1874.

James Auchiah, who was the grandson of Chief Satanta, removed his grandfather's bones from the prison grave and had his body reburied in Oklahoma, eighty-five years after his death. He married Celia Lone Wolf, his childhood sweetheart, granddaughter of the famous Chief Lone Wolf, warrior in arms with Chief Satanta, and became a very famous painter.

Chapter Eight
Indian Wars

In 1778, a Comanche war party attacked the village of Pueblo de Bucareli, in Comanche territory and drove off 200 horses, and destroyed the village. The Spanish colonists killed three of the Comanche warriors,

Ten Bears, a Comanche chief also known as Ten Elks *(Parawahsaymen)*, was born in 1792, was a leader of his people, an eloquent speaker and a peacemaker. He never went on raids as a warrior. He was more a "peace chief." As an elder in the tribe, he was held in high esteem.

Chief Iron Jacket *(Pobishe Guasho)* was also a great chief of the Comanche Nation. He took the name Iron Jacket because he possessed a Spanish coat of mail. He claimed great powers to deflect the white man's bullets with his breath. Iron Jacket fathered a son, named *Pe-ta'-no-ko'-na.* Chief Iron Jacket was the grandfather of another great chief, Quanah Parker.

Peta Nocona *(Petanokona)*, was born around 1825. He was called Nocona, a Comanche chief on the Southern Plains. This chief was greatly feared by the frontier settlers in Texas. Little is known of his upbringing, but he was chief of his fierce *Noconi* band of Comanche Indians

Bent married a Cheyenne Indian named, Owl Woman. In 1828, William Bent, his brothers and partner, Ceran St. Vrain, built an adobe trading post, known as Bent's Fort, on the north bank of the Arkansas River, in what is now La Hunta, Colorado. The walls were four feet thick and 15 feet high with round bastions at two corners. The bastions had canons; cactus on the walls deterred scaling. The fort's dimensions were 135 wide x 180 feet long providing defense from Indians and a supply base. The fort was a stopover on the Santa Fe Trail, a trade route, between

#49.
Comanche Infants in
Cradleboards
Courtesy Western
History Collections,
University of Oklahoma
Libraries

#50.
Cynthia Parker and daughter,
Prairie Flower
Courtesy Footnote.com

Independence, Missouri and Santa Fe, New Mexico. Arapaho, Comanche, Kiowa and Cheyenne Indians traded furs there. It was frequented by John C. Freemont and Army soldiers, who were also stationed there. Kit Carson was a hunter for the fort.

Colonel Henry Dodge and an expedition of dragoons, accompanied by the famous early artist, George Catlin, in July of 1834, rode along the medicine Creek region and were greeted by the Wichita Indians. Sam Houston sent Joseph C. Eldridge into the same region to barter peace with the warring Comanche Indians. Randolph Marcy named Mount Scott after General Winfield Scott, while leading a company of soldiers through the same area, recommended that a post be established near there.

Comanche war parties attacked unprotected farms and ranches on the frontier The Indian braves burned houses and captured their women and children and sold them into slavery as small towns were raided.

Then, in 1834, 60 years after the attack on the Spanish village of Pueblo de Bucareli, the John Parker family built their fort very close to that same location. The Parkers, a prominent Virginia family, settled along the Navasota River, 40 miles east of Waco, Texas. Parkers' Fort was built as a stockade fort, around a cluster of homesteads by the Parker family and their neighbors. It was an outpost on the frontier, near present day, Limestone County in eastern Texas. The Parker family made a big mistake when they settled in Comanche territory.

Arriving in Texas, Silas Parker joined the Texas Rangers and became an officer in 1835. Texas rangers were horse-mounted law officers that ranged the Texas frontier to protect the local citizenry between the Brazos and Trinity Rivers. Elder John Parker was a veteran of the Revolutionary War. Others had fought beside Andrew Jackson in the Battle of New Orleans.

#51. Cynthia Parker's Headstone
Courtesy Footnote.com

#52. "Chief Quanah Parker & His Horse"
Courtesy Footnote.com

The Parkers were very religious people of the Baptist faith and planned to Christianize the pagan Indians. The Parkers believed that they were the elect and that it was God's will that they possess the land. On the contrary, Chief Peta Nocona and the Comanche tribe believed that the "Great Spirit" had created the land for them. The white eyes were encroaching on their land and that meant war. Elder John Parker, his wife, sons and their wives and children and neighbors established Parker's Fort as a defense against Indian attack.

Preparing for war, Comanche warriors prayed to their "Grandfather" (their god) for a successful raid. The Indians painted their faces, bodies and their horses with war paint. They did the war dance for victory and armed themselves with bow and arrows, war-clubs, rifles and lances.

Late in May, 1836, farmers, L.D. Nixon, L.M.T. Plummer and James W. Parker left the fort to work in the fields, near the river, about a mile distant. Ben Parker was standing guard in a field, when he saw the Comanche war party of over 200 warriors. The surprise attack was subtle as the Indians displayed a white flag of peace as they slowly rode in, a ruse to throw the Parkers off guard. Lucy Parker, Mrs. Nixon (Silas' niece) and most of the women, and children ran for the neighbor's farm when they saw the Comanche war party. The warriors confronted and surrounded Benjamin Parker. A number of arrows from the Comanche's bows riddled his body.

Although the fortress was built to ward off wild Indians, the Comanche war party, led by Chief Nocona broke down its defenses and ambushed the immigrants inside Fort Parker. Silas Parker ran to get his shot pouch. The braves shot Robert and Samuel Frost as they attempted to defend the women and children. Elder John Parker and Mrs. Kellogg attempted to escape, but were cut off by the warriors. Cynthia's grandfather

#53.
"Comanche Chieftain"
Courtesy Azusa Publishing
Company, LLC

#54.
"Chief Quanah & Wives"
Courtesy Footnote.com

was scalped alive and dismembered. Before he died her grandmother was molested, then stabbed with a knife and left to die. The Indians killed Elder John and Grandma, Benjamin and Silas Parker, G.E., Dwight, Robert, and Samuel Frost that morning in the Fort Parker massacre.

The frenzied warriors tore the place apart pillaging the fort. As they rode out, the Comanches shot a number of cattle. The attack was fast and furious. The raider's message to others was to stay out of their territory.

The custom was to acquire slaves on a raid. The Comanches captured two women and three children: Rachael Plummer and her young son, James, Elizabeth Kellogg, Silas Parker's six year old son John, and his nine year old daughter, Cynthia Ann. Rachael was pregnant at the time. Ranger Silas shot four Indians, but was killed trying to defend the women and children.

The Comanches rode along the streams of their territory back to the village. We learned that the captives were divided among three Comanche bands. One band stole Rachael Plummer and James Pratt. Another captured Elizabeth Kellogg and the third band took captives, Cynthia and John Parker.

Like many slaves, Rachael Plummer was beaten often by her mistress. When she reached her breaking point, Rachael grabbed the femur bone of a buffalo and beat her tormentor senseless. After that, she became well known to the Comanche's as the woman who dared to fight back.

The Comanche Indians had become slave traders for profit. They rode across the border into Mexican settlements and took slaves of women and children. Females were usually raped. Being accustomed to capturing females in raids for wives and slaves, Comanche braves captured Indian, Mexican and Spanish, as well as Texan women and children.

Occasionally, children were adopted. Slaves were treated either humanely or sometimes cruelly. Young women were taught to carry water and gather wood to be hauled to the camp lodges, like regular Indian girls.

In over a 150-year period it has been estimated that more than 20,000 thousand slaves were captured by the Comanche. They killed more white men and took more slaves of them than any other American Indian tribe.

Women captives, who were ransomed and returned to society, had blank looks on their faces with empty stares, resembling brain wash. Women captives were always raped, as per Comanche custom, and became the property of the warrior abductor. If there was a question of ownership, she became property of the whole Indian band.

Mrs. Plummer was ransomed after twenty one months and rescued from the Indians, as her will was broken. In August of 1837, Rachael Parker Plummer was purchased from the Comanche Indians by Mexican traders, who paid her ransom and actually saved her life. She was subjected to a long, grueling journey along the Santa Fe Trail to Santa Fe, a province of Mexico. Rachael was considered to be the first woman to travel the Santa Fe Trail and the first U.S. citizen to reside in Santa Fe. She was the only survivor of the massacre that lived to tell the story.

In Santa Fe Rachael was sold as a slave to William and Mary Donoho, who were kind to her and took her in. She slept in a bed for the first time in nearly two years. She bore two children there. They raised $150 and promised to send her home to her father, but it was the wrong time.

Revolt broke out in Santa Fe and 2,000 Indians ambushed a compliment of two hundred militiamen, massacring them. The insurgents went on to behead the governor and parade his head through the streets on a pole. A district judge was put in stocks by the rebels and his body mutilated.

On February 19, 1838, after a hard 19 month passage, Rachael Parker Plummer arrived at her father's home in Huntsville. Texas. She was gaunt, scarred by the Comanche Indians. Sadly, Rachael died a year later.

In 1840, Colonel Len Williams and a Delaware Indian guide visited the Comanche encampment four years after Cynthia had been captured and had heard stories of a blue-eyed blonde female held captive in this village.

Chief Pahauka allowed the Colonel to see Cynthia, who tried to speak with her; but she just stared at the ground and did not converse with him. She feared the white men and ran and hid. Cynthia had decided to do anything to stay alive, so she turned Comanche. Williams offered a sizable ransom for the girl, but Pahauka, her Indian father refused the trade and said that it was not enough. Having grown fond of Cynthia, the Comanche people adopted her into the tribe at this time. She would have been around 13.

At the time of the Comanche massacre on Fort Parker, Kit Carson and Will Drannan were trading furs they had trapped in Comanche territory, in a village on the Arkansas River. Carson and Drannan were experienced in fighting the Ute Indians. In 1852, Chief Kiwatchee asked Carson and Drannan to join them in war against the Utes. He declined and said that he would rather observe the fight. The two tribes faced each other, while Comanche drum warriors beat tom-toms; the Comanche braves charged and fought in mortal combat. As the battle ended, the Comanche warriors won. The Comanche warriors counted their wounds as signs of valor.

Chief Pete Nocona took Cynthia for his bride when she turned eighteen years of age. They gave her the Indian name, Nadua (Someone Found). She was one of several wives, being the Comanche tribe practiced

#55.
"Comanche Chief
Quanah Parker"
Courtesy Footnote.com

#56. Quanah Parker's
Two Daughters
Courtesy Azusa Publishing
Company, LLC

polygamy. It seems ironic that Cynthia Anne became the bride of the one whose war party killed her family. She must have blanked everything out.

Sometime around 1850, Quanah was born in a tipi in the Wichita Mountains, being destined to become Chief of the Comanche Nation. He was the firstborn of three children. Quanah had a younger brother, named Pena, (sweet as honey), sometimes called Pecos, and a little sister, called Topsana or Prairie Flower. Chief Nocona was pleased with Cynthia for bearing him three offspring; the Comanche normally suffered from a low birthrate. One author attributed the low rate of birth to the women who were always in the saddle, causing miscarriages and limiting child births.

Government officials, P.M. Butler and M.G. Lewis located Cynthia Parker and her brother John in a Comanche village located at the head of the Wichita River. They offered a king's ransom for her, goods plus $400-500.00 cash, but Cynthia only ran and hid from them, in fear. By then, she was already married to Chief Nocona. On August 8, 1846, they wrote to the Commissioner of Indian Affairs that they had rescued one white slave and three Mexican youth from slavery, but they couldn't save the Parker children.

Quanah rode with his mother, as a baby and was in the saddle, as soon as he learned to walk. After that he had a pony of his own and by the time he was a teenager, was an expert horseman and skilled archer in the use of the bow and arrow. He could wield a knife, spear and tomahawk. Young Quanah grew into a muscular six foot warrior with steel grey eyes. By the time that he was 15 years of age, Quanah had counted coup by taking an enemy's life.

Bent's Fort thrived for over twenty years, when business fell off. William Bent attempted to sell the fort to the government for some time and became frustrated. By failure, so he dynamited and abandoned the fort in 1849. Bent built a new, smaller version of the first fort 38 miles downstream. A century later, the U.S. Park Service rebuilt the fort on its old foundation.

Around 1850, De Shields and a party of white hunters met Cynthia Parker on the prairie along the Upper Canadian River and offered to pay her ransom; some of the hunters were friends of the Parkers. They asked her if she wanted to return to her family. Young Cynthia pointed to her children and shook her head, no. Although she could not speak English, Cynthia signed that she had children and a husband that she loved very much.

In 1850, Chief Peta Nocona, Quanah and the Noconi (wanderers) band were hunting buffalo, making jerky and tanning hides, when 40 Texas Rangers and 21 U.S. Calvary, under Captain Lawrence Sullivan Ross attacked. They took the Comanche village at Pease River by surprise. Ross had been on the trail of Peta Nocona ever since the Parker massacre. They took a blue-eyed Caucasian girl captive. She spoke no English. It was common knowledge that Cynthia Parker was being held captive by the Comanches.

Her Uncle Isaac was summoned and positively identified her as his niece. Isaac took her back to eastern Texas to live with the Parkers. Reunited with the Parker family, she attempted to escape and return to the Comanche world, but was caught and restrained.

Quanah was just 25 when he led his first war party. He learned that he was a half-breed and came under scrutiny for it. When his father, Peta Nocona died of an old injury, Quanah initiated and organized his own composite band of Comanches and became their chief. Young Quanah Parker became the head chief of the Quahadi (Antelope) band of the Comanche Indians; they were the fiercest Indian warriors on the Southern Plains.

57.
Cheyenne Sun Dancers
Courtesy Azusa Publishing
Company, LLC

#58.
Offerings to the Sun
Courtesy Azusa Publishing
Company, LLC

The chief had to be a good hunter and mighty warrior, to become favorite of the people. It also helped that he was a good speaker. Quanah led his own war party and managed to execute a raid and then disappear to elude the U.S. Army. Quanah took Weakeah, daughter of Comanche Chief Yellow Bear and then took four more wives and fathered 25 children all together.

Chief Quanah told the story passed down from legend of how his tribe came to be called the Snake Indians. The neighboring tribes referred to the Shoshoni by using the universal sign language of a slithering hand motion. This described how the Snake Indians would vanish behind rocks like "Snakes going backwards" and reappear to fight again.

By 1850, the Comanche had amassed such large herd of horses, that they had a surplus. Estimates have been made of the Comanche Indians owning as many as 50,000 horses at that time. Commerce was lucrative among the Indian natives. They rode hundreds of miles to raid for horses. Comanche Indians built massive herds of horses, as tribal wealth. One warrior could own 250 horses. Chief Quanah was said to have over 1,000 head in his personal herd. Horses were used as trading stock.

The Cheyenne Indians possessed beads, blankets, brass kettles, calico, guns and ammunition, garnered from bartering with trade forts to trade. The Apache, Comanche and Kiowa Indians brought horses for trade with the southern Cheyenne Indians.

In 1853, a number of Comanche warriors returned to their old haunts. The status of Comanche women had deteriorated, as agriculture was abandoned and warfare took its place as the norm. Gold miners in Colorado, 1850-60's clamored over Indian land, by the thousands. By 1858, tension ran high among the Indians.

Four southwestern Indian tribes banned together in a peaceful socio-political alliance against the white man. The allied tribes voted

Quanah Parker, son of a white captive and a Comanche chief, as their leader and war chief. In the 1860's, Chief Quanah led the Comanche, Kiowa, Kiowa-Apache and Southern Plains Arapaho against the white-eyes. Chief Quanah mounted on his black stallion, at the head of a band of several hundred whooping Indian warriors, struck fear in the eyes of the enemy.

In 1860, the U.S. Army sent three columns of troops to fight the Arapaho, Cheyenne, Comanche and Kiowa Indians, who had closed the Santa Fe Trail.

Cynthia Parker never adjusted to their way of life; heart-broken, she died in 1861. Her husband, Peta Nocona also died the same year, of an old wound. Their love evolved under strange circumstances, but apparently was true love. Their deaths troubled Quanah and brother, Pecos, also died of disease.

In 1861, America began the Civil War during Abraham Lincoln's presidency. Tragically, the south waged war against the north and brother fought against brother. The war was fought mainly over slavery, which was favored in the south. There were 11 slave states in the south that had seceded from the Union; they formed the Confederate States of America or the Confederacy, led by General Jefferson Davis.

The Union, in the north was comprised of 23 free States, that had abolished slavery and 5 border-states. 700,000 soldiers died during the War Between the States. While the Civil War raged, the Indian Wars were fought in the south west, while the Army and top generals were committed, with few soldiers on the western front.

In 1863, there was a full-scale war on the Great Plains, with the fore-mentioned tribes plus the Kiowa-Apache.

Ten Bears was voted by the tribe, as a delegate to the peace conferences. In 1863, he visited Washington D.C. to represent the

Comanche tribe, but gained no concessions from the government. The Comanche Indians were forced to sign away their lands and accept reservation life, but they preferred their old days and ways.

During the war on the Southern Plains, marauding Comanche and Kiowa war parties continued making vicious raids on white settlements. Quanah and his Quahadi band were relentless in their attacks.

Settlers were murdered, their women and children were captured for slaves and wives and their horses and livestock were stolen. Chief Quanah Parker led war parties into Mexico and raided there, where they also took captives. The Kiowa Indian war parties raided into Mexico, also under Chief Lone Wolf.

Aided by the horse, the Comanche army was nearly unbeatable and became, "Lords of the Southern Plains." As war leader of the combined tribes, Quanah and his braves entered into combat with the 4th Cavalry, the Spanish Army, Mexican Army and Texas Rangers in the Comanche Wars. At the same time they warred with other Indian tribes.

Christopher "Kit" Carson was born a tiny baby, so his parents called him Kit. He worked as an apprentice and a herder, which took him to Santa Fe and to Taos, New Mexico, a town that became home to him.

He learned Indian customs, languages and to sign, while trapping for furs in the Rockies. At the "1835 Rendezvous," Carson was challenged to a horse-mounted duel by a bully French fur trapper, named Shunar, over a gorgeous Arapaho Indian maiden named, *Waanike*. Carson shot Shunar and won Waanike for his wife; she bore him two children, before dying young.

Carson signed up as guide for John C. Freemont. Kit married Josepha Jaramillo, his true love, in 1843. For four years Carson and Freemont blazed the Oregon Trail, crossing over America three times.

He rode dispatch to Washington D.C. In the New Mexico area, he was appointed Indian Agent to the Ute Indians for 10 years. They loved Carson and called him "Father Kit." During the Civil War, he had attained the rank of Brigadier General.

In 1864, the Comanche and Kiowa Indians were attacking stage coaches and wagon trains bound for Santa Fe, New Mexico. U.S. Army General James H. Carleton ordered Colonel Christopher Carson, who commanded the 1st Cavalry of New Mexico Volunteers, into the interior to engage the warring Indians somewhere south of the Canadian River.

The first Battle of Adobe Walls occurred on November 25, 1864, when Colonel Christopher "Kit" Carson engaged the Comanche, Kiowa and Kiowa-Apache in war. Carson built up an army of 14 officers, 321 enlisted men and 75 Ute and Jicarilla Apache scouts and soldiers from Lucien Maxwell's ranch, near Cimarron, New Mexico. Two howitzer canons were under the command of Lt. George Pettis, 27 wagons and an ambulance. They had 45 days of rations. Due to heavy snowfall, Carson had left Lt. Col. Abreau in command of the Infantry and supply train as back up.

Colonel Carson headed the march toward Adobe Walls, where there was a winter camp of Comanche and Kiowa Indians, on the Texas panhandle, where Kit had spent time working at Bent's Fort 20 years earlier. His scouts saw a large body of Indians, horses and cattle mingling around Adobe Walls.

No talking or warming cooking fires were allowed on November 25 and around 8:30 a.m., Carson's command attacked Chief Dohasan's Kiowa village of about 150 lodges and routed them from their village.

#59. "Christopher "Kit" Carson
Courtesy Azusa Publishing Company, LLC

Word of the attack spread, as Carson moved his Army toward Adobe Walls. An encampment of 500 Comanche lodges and several thousand warriors was more than Col. Carson had planned on. Many random attacks by the Comanche braves came. Pettis' howitzers held the warriors at bay.

Chief Dohasan led many attacks, as did Chief Satanta and Chief Stumbling Bear. It must have been somewhat of a comical sight to see Satanta, in the army uniform General Custer had given him answering Carson's bugler's call with his own trumpet he had taken off a dead soldier.

Rations were running low and Colonel Carson called a retreat, knowing that they were outnumbered by several thousand Indians. The Comanche braves realized this and started brush fires, burning toward them to block their retreat. Carson countered by moving to higher ground by lighting fires, also and continued fire.

Carson gave the order to burn the Kiowa and Kiowa-Apache lodges, as it turned twilight. Kiowa Chief Iron Shirt refused to leave his teepee and died in the fire. Robes, weapons and rations were destroyed in the fire. Colonel Carson continued his retreat. Low on supplies, he expected to reconnoiter with Lieutenant Colonel Abreau's column, coming from Mule Springs. The two forces united and camped for the night. The next day they rode to Fort Bascom and disbanded.

In four days Colonel Carson had won a great victory. The Indians lost around 150 warriors dead and 175 lodges. Carson's loses were three dead and 25 wounded, three died later. A young Mexican volunteer took an Indian's scalp.

Carson fought 2,000 Comanche and Kiowa in the Texas panhandle area, second only in volume to George Armstrong Custer in 1876 at

Custer's Last Stand. Carson's wife, Josepha, died and Kit passed away one month later, in 1868. The Second Battle of Adobe Walls would occur in ten years.

Black Kettle was chief of a band of 600 Southern Cheyenne and Plains Arapaho Indians. Black Kettle informed Fort Lyons where his tribe's village was located, 40 miles north of Fort Lyons. He was a peace chief and had spoken to the Army about peace and flew an American Flag and a white flag over his lodge. Black Kettle and his warriors were on a buffalo hunt.

Colonial Chivington reported to Fort Lyons and was informed that Chief Black Kettle had already surrendered, but Chivington disregarded the news and rode ahead of his column toward Black Kettle's village. Black Kettle thought they were at peace, but still the Cavalry came.

Five days after the Battle of Adobe Walls, on November 29, 1864, Colonel Chivington and 700 Colorado volunteers attacked and massacred the sleeping village of Cheyenne Indian women and children. It was a cowardly act. Chivington knew this but advanced, taking pleasure in the moment.

Angry war parties of Plains Arapahos and Southern Cheyenne Indian warriors attacked mining camps, stage-lines and wagon trains. A pioneer family outside of Denver was killed by those warriors. That Indian War was called the Cheyenne–Arapaho War or the Colorado War of 1864-65.

Colorado Territory Governor John Evans wanted the Indians hunting ground for white settlement. The Indians refused to sell. Governor Evans asked Lieutenant Colonel John Covington to stop the Indian violence.

Covington was known to hate the Indians, who wanted to see them eradicated. He enjoyed attacking the Arapaho, Comanche, Kiowa and Sioux villages, razing them to the ground, in early Colorado and Kansas.

Comanche warriors hunted and went on the war trail across the Texas frontier, religiously. Their hunting and going on raids clouded the perception of Indians living on the reservation. The idea of staying on the reservation and drawing winter rations from the agency, before going out during the summer to raid and hunt buffalo was not working. There was peace in winter and bloodshed in the summer.

Fetterman's Outpost, on the Bozeman Trail and Elliot's Squadron, on the Wichita River in 1868were wiped out by Comanche attacks. Frustrated, General Sherman ordered that his officers should wipe out as many Indian camps as possible, in order to reduce their numbers.

With the Civil War over, the Army roles were greatly reduced down to 25,000 officers and enlisted men in 1869 left to fight the Indian Wars. The rag-tag U.S. Army was undisciplined. Half of the recruits deserted, rather than report to fight Indians.

The Indians complained of the lack of firearms to hunt to provide ample food, so the Department of the Interior delivered several tons of guns and ammunition to the Plains Indians, although it was illegal under federal law to sell guns to the Indians.

Many of the guns delivered were new-model repeating Spencer and Henry rifles, while the U.S. Army carried older single- shot models. The Plains Indians became better equipped than the Army, courtesy of the American government. Now they could hunt and raid to their heart's content.

Quanah led his Quahadi band and traveled far out on the Southern Plains to hunt the buffalo. They avoided the white man, his society, culture, soldiers, settlements and disease. They made exception and raided the settlements. The Quahadis stayed isolated, the best they could.

While some tribes raided from Texas into Kansas, Chief Quanah led war parties south into Mexico. Other Comanche bands waged war into Kansas and Texas. Federal law prevented Indians being arrested unless they were on reservations with the agent's permission.

They continued to fight the Ute Indians. They hunted the buffalo and traded the hides to the Mexican traders for guns and ammunition who also provided the Comanche with a new incentive, ten-shot lever action repeating rifles. The Comanche Indians had progressed from the primitive bow and arrow to modern weaponry in a few short years. The repeating rifles were a definite advantage to the Comanches in war.

In 1874, a Comanche prophet, named *Ishatai* (White Eagle), a Quahadi medicine man, had a sacred vision of the white man being driven from the Southern Plains, forever by Comanche warriors and the buffalo would return if they did the Sun Dance, which they had never performed before. Warriors who danced the Sun Dance were supposedly given powers of resistance by the gods for protection from white man's bullets.

White Eagle directed the Sun Dance. Several bands participated in the first and last Sun Dance in 1874. The ordeal was common among the Plains Indians. The Comanche Indians were a tribe that performed the Sun Dance only once. It varied from other Sun Dances.

The ceremony was sanctioned in visions or dreams by the medicine man, Ishatai. The festival was held in mid-summer and lasted eight days; it represented birth, life, death and rebirth in the universe.

The first four days was for gathering materials. The last four days was for dancing and celebration; four is a division of eight and a perfect number among the Indians. The Sun Dance was held long ago, but nothing about the Comanche Sun Dance is now remembered.

Adobe Walls, in the Texas panhandle, was an abandoned fort that the buffalo hunters used as their headquarters and for rendezvous. They were led by Colonel Ranald McKenzie, a famous Indian fighter.

Quanah had petitioned the chiefs of the Arapaho, Kiowa and Southern Cheyenne tribes to smoke the pipe to war on the whites and avenge the death of an old friend at the hands of the troops and their Tonkawa Indian scouts.

At the same time he was tired of the white-eyes that had killed off the bison for only the hides and tongues, leaving the meat to rot. Chief Quanah spoke to his warriors of the waste and they decided to avenge the wrongs. He felt it best to go on a night raid and stage a surprise attack on the buffalo hunters. The Comanche Chief met with all of the allied tribes in the immediate area and asked for their support on the war trail against the whites.

The Comanche medicine man, *Ishatai* told them that the war party would conquer and that his magic would bring back the buffalo. He described war-paint that would stop the white man's bullets. Ishatai claimed that Indian horses painted with his magic yellow paint were protected from arrows and bullets. Quanah took old Ishatai along on the raid for his magical powers.

So on June 27, 1874, Chief Quanah Parker formed his war party of allied tribes of some 700 Arapaho, Cheyenne, Comanche and Kiowa braves and rode to Adobe Walls to attack the "white-eyes" buffalo hunters. It was only a just a mile from the ruins of the original Adobe Walls site.

Kiowa Chiefs Lone Wolf and Woman's Heart and their warriors followed Quanah and set out to fight the buffalo hunters at Adobe Walls. Peace-Chief Kicking Bird kept nearly half of the Kiowas from going to war.

Chief Quanah led the massive war party, as they swarmed down on Adobe Walls with only twenty three buffalo hunters, who were holed

117

up in the fort. The sound was deafening, as the thunder of hoof-beats, rifle cracks and war whoops filled the air. Seven hundred Indian warriors attacked the fort.

About 100 yards from the fort on the first charge, a bullet from a buffalo hunter's long-rifle shot his horse out from under Chief Quanah and a second bullet hit the Chief. The Indians' carbine rifles were no match against the buffalo hunter's sharps rifles. The attack was short-lived and a loss.

During the battle, a bullet from a plainsman's long-rifle struck Ishatai's horse right between the eyes, killing it. His magic yellow paint did not protect his mount from the sniper's bullet. He claimed that his medicine had gone because the warriors had killed a skunk, which he forewarned was taboo. Never-the-less, Ishatai lost all credence with his band.

With nine Indians slain and only four buffalo hunters dead, the warriors retreated. A 700 warrior army could have easily wiped out the white-men with a frontal attack, but the Indians did not like the close quarters. Ishatai had spoken with a forked tongue. The shaman's magic did not help them and they lost faith in him. Nine warriors were killed and only four hunters. The fight was named "The Second Battle of Adobe Walls." Some believed it should have been named "The Buffalo Wars," since the Comanche fought over government laws passed to exterminate the buffalo.

Chief Quanah led the Quahadi band on the war trail in Texas. Simultaneously, Arapaho, Cheyenne, Comanche and Kiowa Indian raiders attacked white settlements from Kansas to the New Mexico region. The Indian Wars fought along the Red River in Texas was referred to as "The Red River Wars of 1874-75."

They fought the buffalo hunters, Texas Rangers and the U.S. Army on the Southern Plains. The Comanche Indians and their allies raided on the frontier, attacking stage coach lines, ranches and wagon trains. Public opinion in eastern newspapers condemned the Indian attacks and demanded results from the Army to restore the peace.

During the autumn of 1874, Colonel Ranald Mackenzie led the 4th cavalry to defeat the warring Comanche Indians in Palo Duro Canyon, in the Texas panhandle. Although the Cavalry killed only four Comanche braves, they destroyed blankets, jerky and supplies. The Troops captured and slaughtered 1,400 of the Indians' horses, burning all their lodges.

Chief Quanah and the Comanche warriors escaped with their lives, and saw the smoke from their burning teepees rise in the sky as they retreated. Mackenzie had dealt a deadly blow to the Comanche braves and now their fighting days were numbered. He had defeated them. They were doomed to leave the plains. The last siege on the High Plains was in 1875.

The Comanche Indians were familiar with Colonel Ranald Mackenzie, who operated from Fort Sill. When he ordered the Indians to come in to the fort unconditionally, the band of starving Comanche Indians straggled in to Fort Sill on a hot summer day of June in 1875.

When the majority of the Comanche Indians surrendered at Fort Sill, Oklahoma, Chief Quanah Parker was not among them. He retreated deeper into the frontier, where they managed to survive the harsh winter exposed to the elements.

Quanah Parker finally came in to Fort Sill, after signing the Treaty of Medicine Lodge and surrendered in 1875, after leading the last band of Comanche Indians on the plains. Chief Parker and 400 warriors were the last to relent. On June 2, 1875, Quanah and his Antelope band of Comanche Indians entered Fort Sill, driving 1500 head of horses.

Quanah's band of Comanche Indians surrendered and agreed to dwell on the reservation. The buffalo were nearly gone; the beaver were trapped out and their weapons were confiscated. The Army shot all their horses and life as they had known it had passed. The reign of the "Lords of the Southern Plains" was no more. It was the end of an era for them.

On the reservation, Quanah switched hats and proved to be an excellent financier and politician in the white man's world. He sold grazing rights on the three million acre reserve with leasing fees going to his people from cattle barons.

Quanah was a peaceable chief and was treated with respect by the Army. He had fought bravely to save his people. Quanah transitioned to civilized life quite well. He became a wealthy rancher on the reservation and never forgot his people. Quanah pushed for their education. He promoted leasing of surplus reservation land for raising stock of confederated tribes.

The Chief was appointed Judge of Indian Affairs in 1886. The white men attempted to get the Comanches to divide their reservation into allotments and then sell to them. Quanah Parker traveled to Washington D.C. to change that policy. Indian agents tried to control the Comanche people by gifting and praising them and punished leaders that refused to do the agents wishes.

The Native American Church movement was founded by Quanah Parker about 1890, among the Comanche Indians and spread to other tribes. Members used peyote (hallucinogenic cactus buttons) in their divination. Quanah Parker promoted the church and taught his people the "peyote road" led the Indians to Jesus Christ, through visions. The sacrament of the shaman was eating the peyote cactus button, raw, portraying wolves

#60.
"Rancher Quanah,"
Courtesy Western
History Collections,
University of Oklahoma
Libraries

#61.
"Quanah the Businessman"
Courtesy Footnote.com

eating the heart of the deer (creator). Shaman identified diseases for healing purposes.

The Spanish-American War was fought in 1898. America won and a treaty was signed. In 1907, Oklahoma joined the union and the tribes-people in Indian Territory lost their independence, becoming citizens of Oklahoma.

Quanah established the "Comanche Whitehouse," a 12 room residence, near Fort Sill, Oklahoma with the help of his friend, cattle baron Burke Burnett.

Quanah occasionally wore business suits and was a celebrity. He was invited to appear in Teddy Roosevelt's Inaugural parade in 1905. Quanah died on February 21, 1911, at the age of 64, under the care of a Comanche medicine man in Cache, Oklahoma and was buried beside his mother, Cynthia Ann Parker, whose body had been reinterred there. Two of his wives survived him. In his lifetime, Quanah claimed eight wives and 25 children, a true Comanche. He remained polygamous and used traditional peyote.

Quanah has been called the "Last Comanche Chief." He was to be the most influential Comanche chief, ever. Chief Quanah Parker was the greatest Comanche War-chief. Descendants of both white and Indian Parkers still keep in touch and have family reunions. Quanah, Texas was named for the Chief.

The Native American Church was incorporated in Oklahoma in 1918, as a non-profit organization, as the Native American Church, but the Navajo Tribal Council declared the church illegal in 1940 and believed it harmful to Navaho Christians and their culture. The church then continued underground until 1967, when it reversed its identification. Church membership grew to 50,000, in America, Canada and Mexico by 1966.

Chapter Nine
Texas Rangers

Texas was a northern province of Mexico that was being colonized by white immigrants. San Antonio began as an Indian village in a spring-fed wooded area in the Texas hills. A Catholic father named the site for the Feast Day of Saint Anthony de Padova. Spain established the San Antonio de Bexar Mission there in 1718. It became the home to missionaries and Indian converts, who worked the land.

This was later the site of the Alamo Mission, a Spanish name for cottonwood. A civil villa was established there in 1731. San Antonio was founded as a Spanish settlement; it became a Mexican fortress until the Texas Revolution.

The Comanche Indians had control of the Southern Plains and were a relentless foe. They attacked anyone in their territory, Spaniards, Mexicans, Texans or Indians. Harmon Hays had fought the British with Andy Jackson and Sam Houston in 1814.

Stephen Austin established the town of San Antonio. A Virginian, Stephen Fuller Austin was known as the "Father of Texas." His father, Moses Austin, traveled to Spanish Texas and started to establish settlement there, but passed on. Stephen continued his work. He founded the first Anglo colony in the province of Texas that later became a republic.

Austin traveled to Mexico City and with much diplomacy attained permission and authority to colonize, with him as administrative authority. He selected a site along the Brazos and Colorado Rivers and offered Americans land packages to a number of acres for 300 families to settle and pay twelve and one half cents an acre. He settled the incoming colonists into a site along the Brazos and Colorado Rivers by January 1822. Austin set up immigration laws and a judicial system. Mexican law offered 4,428 acres to married men who worked the land and paid the state of Coahuila, Mexico $30.00 in six years.

In 1823, due to the threat of constant Indian attacks, a call for Rangers was made. Some citizens of Texas had acted as vigilantes to protect the people on the frontier from Indian attack and desperados. On May 5, 1823, Lieutenant Moses Morrison mustered ten men to protect a colony. Stephen Austin offered to pay Ranging Men $15.00 a month from his land holdings. The fighting unit ranged the Texas frontier. A plan was formulated to raise a company of 20-30 mounted men to range the frontier, which was the beginning of the Texas Rangers. Men were needed badly to fight in the Texas Indian Wars.

The Mexican government in 1824 established a federal constitution. The Texas colonists struggled under Mexican rule and finally tried to spark rebellion in eastern Texas in 1826. In 1835, the constitution was annulled and replaced by a centralized dictatorship.

March 11, 1824, the U.S. States Secretary of War created a Bureau of Indian Affairs within the War Department. On May 28, 1830, the U.S. Congress passed a bill for the removal of all of the American Indians living east of the Mississippi River. During the next 20 years over 50 American Indian tribes were displaced from their homeland and marched west to "Indian Territory" in Oklahoma.

Austin, Texas was founded by Stephen Austin. The Mexican governor gave Austin the authority of civil and military rule in Austin and authority for a paid militia, there. The forefathers that founded the city of Austin first sought out good solid citizens. They looked for a higher class of people to settle there. Regardless, there were carpet-baggers, hustlers and thieves that moved into the region.

#62.
Jim Bowie
Courtesy Footnote.com

#63.
William Travis
Courtesy Footnote.com

Slavery had been banned in 1824, yet in 1827 Austin lobbied for slaves in Texas. Austin began recruiting families to move to Texas, reaching 900 by 1829. The Mexican government tried to limit immigration by Americans into San Antonio and in 1830 passed laws to stop it. Austin continued the influx, yet Mexico had the authority.

Farmers and ranchers on the frontier were mostly southerners that had migrated west to Texas. They raised cattle, corn and cotton, mainly. There were Mexican rancheros along the Rio Grande River that raised cattle and sheep. In 1832-1833, Texas colonists tried to declare their independence from Mexico. The immigration ban was lifted, but independence was denied.

In 1834, the U.S. government intervened to stop the Indian War and negotiated a peace between the Comanche Indians and the eastern tribes in Comancheria. The Comanches signed, but were not happy. Even though they respected the agreement, they did not like strangers in their territory.

The Southern Plains became a land of bloodshed because warfare broke out again. The Indian War in Texas raged for 40 years. The Texas cowboys, ranchers, and sodbusters on the frontier faced the grim possibility of wild Indians, who might appear and attack at any time. Members of their families faced the possibility of loss of life or capture by the Indians, as well as stealing their livestock. The Comanche had long resisted the white man's intrusion on their land. They treated all intruders as enemies and won nearly all of their battles to defend their territory.

Samuel Houston was nick-named the "Raven." The name was given him, as an adolescent, by the Cherokee Indians; he formed close ties with them. Sam joined the Army under "Andy" Jackson in the Creek Indian Wars (1813-1814). He later resigned his commission and was

#64. Sam Houston
Courtesy Footnote.com

appointed Adjutant General of Tennessee, served two terms of Congress (1823-27) and was elected Governor of Tennessee in 1827. Houston married Eliza Allen on January 1, 1829, but the marriage was dissolved and he resigned his post, when pressured by Allen's family.

For the next six years, Houston lived among the Cherokee Indians in Indian Territory (Oklahoma). He later took an Indian wife, Tiana Rogers, and had become a Cherokee citizen. Houston acted as a trader, advisor and special envoy for the Cherokee tribe.

Sam Houston was commissioned by Andrew Jackson as negotiator to the Texas Comanche Indians. He went to Texas to hold council and make peace with the Comanche Indians. Sam believed that if the Comanche Indians were treated honestly and fairly that they would be peaceable. He held council with the Comanche tribunal and in time, a treaty was signed.

The agreement read that the Comanche warriors would discontinue raids on the Texans and the settlers would avoid Comancheria. Although Sam Houston bartered peace with the Comanche Indians, the legislature refused to form a boundary between Comancheria and the Republic of Texas. Later, when the treaty became law, things got worse.

In 1835, the towns of Sonora, Chihuahua and Durango, Mexico reestablished bounties for Comanche Indian scalps. It was again open season on Comanche Indians.

Colonel William B. Travis led the volunteers on an attack on Anahuac. Captain Antonio Tenorio surrendered the post. Stephen Austin returned from imprisonment in Mexico and was given a position as Chairman of Safety and Correspondence in San Felipe.

While citizens of the Republic wanted Texas annexed to the United States, General Santa Anna had other ideas concerning occupying Coahuila and Tejas (Texas), under his military dictatorship. General Martin

#65. Texas Rangers Fight the Comanches
Artist unknown, Courtesy Dreamstime.com

Perfecto de Cos landed at Copano Bay with 500 soldiers and marched to San Antonio. Cos announced his intention to run all of the settlers out of Texas and that he would punish those responsible for the attack on Anahuac. The next day fighting broke out and the Texas Revolt began in October of 1835 with the battle at Gonzales. The Battle of the Siege of Bexar was also fought in 1835.

On February 23, 1836, Mexican General Santa Anna and his 2400 man Army of Mexican regulars swept north from Mexico City and stormed the Alamo, once a deserted mission outside of (San Antonio de Bexar), now present day San Antonio. Inside, holed up in the old mission, under the command of Colonel William B. Travis, and co-commander, Jim Bowie, famous knife manufacturer, and the famous Davy Crockett with his fighting men of Tennessee, around 200 patriots, that had dug in.

The fighting was heavy. Colonel Travis' only hope was reinforcements, under Colonel Fannin, but they never came. Santa Anna's fighting Infantry and Cavalry were well trained and his big canons and artillery hammered the fortress. Smoke and fire filled the air. The stench of death and acrid, blue smoke from rifle and canon fire was stifling. The gallant men fought bravely for their lives and held the Mexican Army off for 12 days during the terrible siege.

Sadly, as General Santa Anna called the cease-fire, on March 6, William B. Travis, Jim Bowie, Colonel David Crockett and nearly 200 brave men had died in a blaze of glory, save two that lived. Some four-six hundred Mexican regulars died or were wounded. During the melee, while the Texas volunteers fought for their lives, the Texas Republic wrote a new constitution of independence, on March 2, 1836.

During the Texas Revolution, Sam Houston went to Texas, while it was still under Mexican rule. Houston was named the Commanding

General of the Republic Army when Texas was declared to be an independent republic.

After the massacre at the Alamo, an even more heinous act was performed by the evil dictator, General Antonio Lopez de Santa Anna in the town of Goliad, Texas, near the Gulf of Mexico, three weeks later.

Santa Anna's Army over 2,000 dragoons defeated the Texas Republic Army in battle. Three hundred and fifty brave Texans surrendered to the coward, Santa Anna. The monster general cruelly ordered the prisoners marched into the street and executed by his firing squads, as an example. They were gunned down and their bodies burned.

Six weeks later, the courageous Texans, fighting under Sam Houston, stopped Santa Anna. (Houston was in command at the Battle of Jacinto Creek and led the charge crying, "Remember the Alamo!".) The rebels managed a resounding victory, April 21, 1836. Santa Anna was captured the next day. As a result of the Texas Revolution, in 1836 Texas declared its independence from Mexico.

On August 4, 1836, Austin announced his candidacy for President of the Republic. Two weeks before the election, Houston entered the race and won the victory as President. He appointed Austin as his Secretary of State. In December 1836, Stephen Austin caught cold, developed a high fever and contacted pneumonia.

On December 27, 1836, he died. Hearing of Austin's death, Houston said, "the Father of Texas is no more; the first pioneer of the wilderness has departed." He was later buried in Austin.

The Republic of Texas formed the Texas Rangers, who mobilized and rode together during the years of the Texas Republic from 1836-1845. The job performed was called a ranging service and therefore the name, Texas Rangers. The Texas Rangers were a special branch of the police force that began as a semi-official group of mounted citizens, who were made up of a young bunch of riders, who were energetic wranglers with horse savvy.

An act of the Texas legislature on June 12, 1837 authorized the Texas Rangers to employ members of friendly Indian tribes as scouts and spies. These were usually from the eastern tribes that had migrated to Indian Territory: the Cherokee, Choctaw, Delaware, Shawnee and Seminole Indians. In 1838, Texas and the Comanche Indians signed a peace treaty.

The Lipan Apache and the Tonkawa Indians had frequently accompanied the Rangers into battle with the Comanche Indians, their enemies and also served as scouts.

Ranger companies were called mounted volunteers, mounted gunman, spies and minutemen and were to range the frontier, protect settlers from Indian raids and lawlessness. Rangers signed on for a number of days or months. The pay was poor, usually in promissory notes or nearly worthless Republic money. Rangers receiving little pay instead divided their spoils from raids, mostly horses, among them. Captain had trouble finding recruits.

The job of the Texas Rangers was to protect the citizenry on the Texas frontier. As protection from Comanche raids, they were organized to fight Indians and keep the peace. The Texas Rangers used the same technique as the Spanish Army and attacked the Comanche Indians in their territory.

This strategy worked and they succeeded. The Texas Rangers were unique lawmen, who upheld the laws of Texas, fought desperados, Indians and Mexican bandits, in the name of "Lone Star" justice in Ranger tradition.

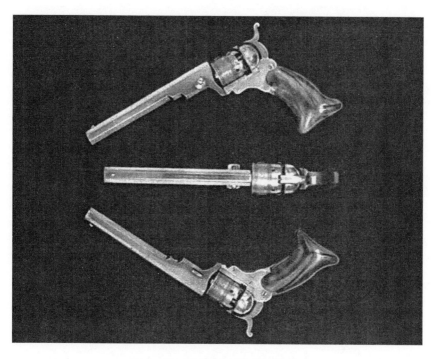

#66. "Colt Patterson Revolver"
Courtesy National Cowboy & Western Heritage Museum

The Rangers had to be rough, tough, two-fisted gunslingers, ready to fight Indians. They could rope, ride and handle a "riata," (lasso). Horses had to be broken so they were also "bronc" riders. They sometimes rode for days and wound up saddle-sore. The Rangers rode the open frontier, slept under the stars and lived off of nature, similar to the Indians.

The Texas lived on wild game that they hunted for subsistence. The Rangers used their saddles for pillows and a bed-roll (saddle blanket) as a bed and slept out under the stars. They wore no special uniform and had no company flag. Their clothing consisted of a red flannel shirt, overhauls, moccasins or boots and a coon-skin cap.

The Republic needed surveyors to plat the land so they hired Rangers and former Rangers as surveyors and deputy surveyors. It was no surprise, when the sons of Harmon Hays, William and his younger brother, Jack arrived at Sam Houston's camp in 1838 to join the Texas Rangers.

Mirabeau Bonaparte Lamar became the second president of the Republic of Texas on December 1, 1838. He was against joining the Union and detested Sam Houston. Lamar relocated the capital of the Republic from Houston to Austin, Texas. Lamar called for war against the warring Comanche Indians and the young Texas Rangers were ready to answer the call.

Jack was named after his father's old commanding officer, Lieutenant John Coffee. They presented a letter from their uncle introducing them as surveyors for service in the Texas Rangers to Sam Houston. Jack stood 5' 8" tall, with a slender build and was smooth-shaven. He had brown hair and was fair complected. Jack was a two fisted, gun-slinging cowboy, who made a hardy Texas Ranger and he formed a militia in 1839.

During the Indian Wars, Ranger Colonel John Moore led a raid on a Comanche Indian encampment near the mouth of the San Saba River in February of 1839. Although the Rangers killed between 30 and 40 Comanche Indians, as they fought, the braves ran off their whole string of horses, forcing them to walk 90 miles back to the settlements.

In 1840, the Cheyenne and Arapaho Indians bartered peace with Comanche, Kiowa and Kiowa-Apache Indians. On March 19, 1840, the Penateka band of Comanche men, women and children came into San Antonio for peace talks with the Texas Rangers.

Among them were 12 Comanche chiefs. The Comanche Indians surrendered a white slave woman that they had taken captive a year earlier. Her name was Matilda Lockhart. Her body was hideously scarred from firebrands, used for her torture by her captors. She spoke and said the chiefs planned to bring one slave at a time for ransom. This riled the Rangers, who were becoming agitated.

The Texas Rangers held council with the chiefs, who represented the Comanche people. As part of their peace plan, the Rangers demanded that the Comanche Indians release all white captives taken in raids. This point was not taken well with the Comanche chiefs, who considered the captives their property. Few agreed, so the Texas Rangers entered the room armed and threatened to hold them until they changed their minds. This was a serious mistake.

Chief Muguara spoke and said that was impossible and that the Comanche believed the white captives were their possessions. He believed no Comanche chief had the authority to order the slaves freed. The chiefs totally refused the Ranger's request.

Their answer was completely unacceptable to the Texas Rangers. The following occurrence was an unavoidable calamity. As a tactic of fear, the Rangers brought soldiers into the council room, brandishing weapons. The chiefs bolted and ran for the door and the soldiers shot them down. They drew knives and fought for their lives, struggling to escape.

Unarmed, they were no match for the soldiers, who had firearms and when the shooting ended, all twelve Comanche chiefs lay dead on the floor. Twenty seven Comanche women and children were taken prisoner. The incident was referred to as the "Council House Massacre" and it confirmed to the Indians that the Texas Rangers could not be trusted.

After the council mishap, it took the Penateka Comanche Indians two full days to sacrifice all of the chiefs horses and bury them. Women ranted and sheared their hair, slashing their limbs in mourning over the dead.

The Rangers gave a woman prisoner a horse and told her to contact the bands and demand that they bring in their captives. A young white boy, who had been a captive and returned to his family, told them, that 13 white captives had been burned at the stake and other white women and children were stripped naked and staked down, purposefully mutilated and killed for revenge. The Comanche raids resumed in more magnitude then before and the Texas Rangers retaliated with their own raids.

Penateka Chief Buffalo Hump was outraged by the killings of the Chiefs of his fellow tribes-people, by the Texas Rangers and vowed to avenge the deaths. Revenge over the Council House massacre came with the rising of the full moon in August of 1840, when 1,000 braves, led by Comanche Chief Buffalo Hump led the Penateka band on the war path.

#67. Quanah Parker's daughter, Wanada
Courtesy Western History Collections
University of Oklahoma Libraries

This uprising was called the "Great Raid of 1840." Chief Peta Nocona may have been on this raid with his band.

The war trail took them south to the cities of Victoria and Linneville, (a leading seaport on the Gulf of Mexico). The frenzied warriors stole all of the horses they could, pillaged and burned the buildings in the town to the ground. The Comanche braves had killed 21 people and took Mrs. Watts, Mrs. Crosby, her child, and a Negro woman and her child hostage.

Eighty seven Texas Rangers, under Colonel Burleson, accompanied by several Tonkawa Indian scouts that had just ridden from Austin joined with Felix Huston's army of about 110 volunteers. The 200 man army intercepted the Comanche Indians on the trail and the battle began; they fought dismounted and on their horses. The Indians circled them firing. The Rangers in hand-to-hand combat routed the Comanche braves and chased them in a running battle as they retreated for 10 or 12 miles. At the Battle of Plum Creek, near Lockhart, eighty braves were reported killed, but the Indians had captured hundreds of their horses and much plunder.

In 1840, Houston married Margaret Lea in Alabama and fathered eight children. He was elected to a second term (1841-1844).

On the evening of September 10, 1842, the Mexican Army seized the town of San Antonio, Texas, meanwhile Jack Hays scouted the roads from Mexico with five volunteers.

John Coffee Hays organized a volunteer army with Ranger barracks in San Antonio. Old San Antonio was a small town of around 1,000 people in 1844 on the banks of the San Antonio River. Jack Hays had become an Indian fighter, when stationed in San Antonio. By 1844, Jack had made the rank of captain when in the service of Texas.

It had Spanish architecture and culture: five Franciscan missions, haciendas, churches, commercial buildings, government structures, and residences of adobe and stone. The citizenry wore mostly Spanish attire, being close to the Mexican border.

Hays led a disciplined outfit made famous for carrying an invention of Samuel Colt, the renown five-shot Colt revolver with a nine inch barrel. His Rangers often carried two colts and an extra cylinder. In combat with the Comanche Indians, the Rangers could fire rounds in 40 seconds, much faster than a Comanche warrior could fire an arrow. The action of the Patterson colt save a lot of Ranger's lives.

These revolvers were known as Patterson colts, since they were manufactured at Samuel Colt's factory in Patterson, New Jersey. Samuel Colt had previously supplied his colts to Sam Houston's Navy since 1839.

Techniques of fighting with the Comanche Indians had to be mastered. Comanche horses could outrun the Ranger's horses. A Comanche warrior could fire a number of arrows, while a Texas Ranger was trying to reload his muzzle-loader and single-shot pistol.

One classic fighting tactic of the Comanche Indians was to act like they were frightened and ride away from the Rangers, in order to draw them into a trap of ambush so that they could fire a shower of arrows upon them. When outnumbered, the Rangers dismounted and fought as a single unit from a defensible position. The Rangers also adopted a method of firing in relays. While one group fired, the other group reloaded.

Jack Hays was a superb Texas Ranger and leader of his men. He had purposefully drilled them again and again in marksmanship. This trip, they were equipped with Patterson colts.

On June 8, 1844, Hays and his company of 14 men were riding along a tributary of the Guadalupe River, 50 miles north of San Antonio. Jack stationed several men as a rear guard. Soon, his men reported seeing 10 Comanche Indians behind them, who attempted a ploy to lure the Rangers to follow; but Hays avoided the ambush. They were bold and daring, but outnumbered five to one, yet well armed.

Suddenly, 70 horse-mounted warriors rode hard toward them, (their bodies painted and adorned with full headdresses). They gave out loud shrieks and war cries. The Rangers met the charge and spurred their horses to attack the Comanche's flank.

The Indians turned to make a frontal attack, while Hays ordered the Rangers to circle their horses to meet the charge. The Comanche warriors attacked again and again in waves and pushed the Texas Rangers back with heavy losses. The Indians must have been perplexed, wondering how the Rangers kept firing.

Finally, Hays ordered Gillespie, one of his officers, to kill the chief, which he did, causing the Comanche war party to flee. Jack Hays and 14 men, with their Patterson Colts, had routed the Comanche warriors, who had lost 23 warriors along with 30 who were wounded. Hays had the victory.

It was the Samuel Colt pistol that gave them about a 300% advantage. With extra cylinders they kept firing from the beginning. Fourteen men had held off 75 Comanche warriors, the first time such a small detachment had held off so great a battery of Indians, changing how battles with the Amerinds were fought in the West.

The colt was used by the Republic Navy, the Texas Rangers and in the Seminole War. It was a wonderful invention, but at the end of the Civil War, Samuel Colt went bankrupt.

In 1845, Texas was annexed as a state by the United States of America and President James Polk had forced Mexico into war. As a result, the Mexican Army attacked Zackory Taylor's American troops, under Seth B. Thornton on Texas's southern border, initiating the Mexican-American War.

The defense against marauding Indian raids shifted from the Texas Rangers in 1845, to the U.S. Army, which used the forts as their main defense. The Army offered the Comanche's refuge on reservations, hoping that they wouldn't join the Mexican Army in the Mexican-American War.

The Mexican War between Mexico and the United States began on April 25, 1846, when a group of Mexican soldiers had ambushed American troops, under Captain Seth B. Thornton, along the southern border at the mouth of the Rio Grande.

Some historians argue that United States President James Polk forced Mexico into war by annexing Texas into the union and stationed an army along the border.

Most of the battles were fought on Texas soil. Ranger Jack Hays played a pivotal role in the Mexican War, as did many Texas Rangers and thousands of brave volunteers, who risked their lives to fight.

On May 13, 1846, the U.S. Congress officially declared war on Mexico. The Mexican-American War lasted only five months. In Mexico City, General Santa Anna resigned his command on September 16, 1846. The conflict ended on September 16, 1846, when American General Winfield Scott advanced and occupied Mexico City, Mexico.

Sam Houston was elected to the U.S. Senate in 1846. Later Chief Buffalo Hump met with Sam Houston and made demands that the white man remain east of Edwards Plateau, which was encompassed in

#68. American Indians Observing Westward Wagons
Artist Unknown, Courtesy Dreamstime.com

its entirety in Comancheria. Buffalo Hump signed a peace treaty with the United States government at Council Springs in 1846.

Many campaigns were fought on Mexican soil, while several battles were waged in the American Southwest. Famous people fought for the United States in the Mexican War; P.G.T. Beauregard, Jefferson Davis, Joseph E. Johnson, Robert E. Lee, George B. McClellan, Zachary Taylor, the Texas Rangers and 115,000 volunteers. It is estimated that over 17,000 died in action and possibly 25,000 were wounded or died of disease.

Sam Houston ran for governor on an independent ticket as a Unionist in 1859. Against his wishes, the Texas Congress voted to secede from the Union in that year and Houston was forced out of office in March of 1861. Sam died in Huntsville, on July 26, 1863. The city of Houston, Texas was named after him.

Much bloodshed had occurred in the 1850's due to the constant raids by the Comanche Indians. Hardin R. Runnels, the newly appointed Governor of Texas, was intent on protecting the citizens residing along the frontier from the Indian's attacks. The situation became uncomfortable and laws were later passed for their protection.

January 28, 1858, John S. Ford was assigned command, as Senor Captain John S. Ford over all of the Texas Rangers in the State of Texas. They were stationed in Austin and the Governor ordered Captain Ford to engage and chastise any hostiles in the area. Ford seemed to be most qualified to lead one hundred Texas Rangers into the interior and rout the hostiles. He led his men directly to the Brazos Indian Reservation. Captain Ford's company was fully equipped with 102 men, an ambulance, two wagons and fifteen pack mules.

Agent Ross called the reservation Indians together and got them all riled up over the Comanche raids on the frontier. The Comanches had been their enemy. About one hundred Indians, led by Chief Placido, volunteered. They were Indians representing the Anadarko, Caddo, Tonkawa, and Waco tribes.

Captain Ford, with Ross's Indians met at Cottonwood Springs. The Indians harbored resentment toward the Comanche Indians from the beginning. They headed northward toward the Red River and on to the Washita River, following the 98th parallel. They reached the Washita River the next day and after twenty one days of forced march, they found a buffalo, crippled by Comanche arrows. The arrowheads were extracted from the carcass.

Now, deep in Comanche territory, Captain Ford left the wagons behind and trying not to be discovered, he assigned men to guard them. They were north of the Rio Negro River. They saw Comanche Indian hunters to the north chasing buffalo. The party followed the Comanches, whose ponies were laden with hides and buffalo jerky. Their Indian tracker discovered a small Comanche encampment.

Captain Ford's men attacked the small village at dawn. Those in the Comanche camp were outnumbered and the ambush was successful. The camp was destroyed. The Comanche males were all killed. They preferreddeath to capture. The women and children were taken captive.

A larger camp, with 70 lodges, was seen on the north bank of the Canadian River, near the mouth of Little Robe Creek. A lone Comanche was sighted, riding alone toward camp. The Rangers tried to pursue him, but he evaded them and rode his horse across the river to camp.

#69. "1800's Frontier Conestoga Wagon"
Courtesy Idaho State Historical Library

#70. Frontier Settlers in the 1800's
Courtesy Azusa Publishing Company, LLC

The lone brave gave an outcry, warning the village of attack. He showed the Rangers how to cross the river by his actions. Approaching the village, they crossed the river. From a line of the Comanche warriors, one warrior emerged displaying a white flag, tied to his lance. He wore a buffalo robe and headdress of buffalo horns. The warrior was no other than Chief Iron Jacket.

Realizing it was a trick, the soldiers began firing. The Comanche braves returned fire. During the battle, Chief Iron Jacket turned and caught a bullet from behind and fell from the saddle and died. His coat of mail failed to protect him from the Texas Ranger's bullets. Jim Pock-Mark, an Anadarko Chief had fired the shot that killed him. It was May 12, 1858.

When Iron Jacket fell from his horse, his warriors scattered and ran west from the village. The Rangers pursued them and a running battle followed over a distance of about five miles. Meanwhile, Chief Peta Nocona and several hundred warriors arrived from the north hills.

Ranger Captain Ford had his men form a battle line, as Chief Peta Nocona and his warrior attacked them. The warriors surrounded the village. The fight with Chief Nocona's warriors resulted in seven Comanche braves slain. Private Robert Nickel was killed by a war party of six Comanches.

The private made the mistake of chasing after the fleeing warriors, alone. George W. Pascal was wounded in a wooded area and a Tonkawa Indian was killed, when he ran out of arrows. Only two men were killed and three wounded in both battles. The Rangers captured 300 horses, and 18 women and children were taken captive. Sixty-nine braves were killed. Captain Ford was accused of killing women. He fired back, that it was hard to distinguish the gender of Indians in battle.

Tonkawa Indian scouts fought with the Texas Rangers up until 1850. Then, in 1859, Chief Buffalo Hump led his people onto the Oklahoma reservation at Fort Cobb. The old chief died there in 1870.

Preparing to go on the war trail, *Mam 'an-ti* the Kiowa medicine man predicted that a revenge raid of the war party would be a success and that at least one of the white-eyes would die. He said that one or two white man would be killed by warriors riding gray horses and prophesied that young Hunting Horse would be gifted a fine bay horse. Chief Tah-bone-mah led his band of Kiowa Indians on the war trail, looking for revenge. Mamanti and Loud Talker rode among them. The Kiowa's chased four cowboys, who escaped along the Butterfield Stage Road.

In July of 1860, a band of Texas Rangers followed the cold trail of a Comanche Indian war party headed for Indian Territory. Then the Indians spotted a band of Texas Rangers, who took up the chase, but rode into a trap.

Warriors ambushed the Rangers from both sides, leaving two dead. Chief Lone Wolf was jubilant, believing his son's death had been avenged. In the aftermath, the old medicine man's oracle supposedly came true. Warriors on gray horses did kill the Rangers and Chief Tahbonemah did give the young brave the bay horse, the Ranger who was killed, was riding. Actually, it was probably the medicine man's trickery to retell a story and claim to have foreseen the incident before it happened.

Nelson Lee, a famous Texas Ranger, who was not even 20, was captured by Comanche warriors and held captive for three years. His life was spared because of a pocket watch he carried. Lee was born in 1807, in Brownsville, New York, where he worked as a boats-man and rafts-man on the St. Lawrence River for several years, before sailing around the world.

Nelson traveled to Texas, where he joined the Texas Rangers in 1840, under Captain Cameron, a Scot, in the vicinity of the Rio Grande River, serving under President Sam Houston. Houston's order for the Texas Rangers was to search for marauding bands of Indians and Mexican bandits and desperados on the frontier.

The Rangers had no special uniform; Lee wore overalls, a flannel shirt, moccasins, and a coon-skin cap. He carried two or three revolvers, a rifle and a Bowie-knife. Lee slept under the stars, beneath a saddle-blanket, with a saddle for a pillow and only the howl of a lonesome coyote to put him to sleep.

Lee's first fighting engagement happened when his company of Texas Rangers encountered a band of Comanche warriors near Casa Blanca, not far from the Nueces River. There was an exchange of arrows and bullets when a band of Comanche warriors rode right up to them and got in their faces, counting coup, amid war-whoops, exhibiting their bravery, before retreating.

The next time Nelson Lee would see Comanche warriors, the Texas Rangers gained sight of 700 Comanche braves on the war path that had attacked a white settlement on the Levaca River. Four white men were killed and three of their women captured. The Army was contacted; runners reached General Burleson on the Colorado River. The General, at the time, was waiting for reinforcements.

Nelson Lee ended his six months enlistment under Cameroun and re-enlisted for his second campaign under Jack Hays in San Antonio. Nelson rode a black stallion, named "Black Prince," his favorite horse. Black Prince proved to be a trusted mount in the service. It was loyal and kept up the pace, traveling at top speed.

Lee's unit managed to track down Mexican marauders and Indians on the war path. He faced all kinds of danger in his years in the service. Nelson rejoined the Texas Rangers on many occasions, during his career. He served as a soldier and at times a spy. Lee reenlisted a third time in 1842.

Between 1844 and 1846, Lee worked as a herder of horses and a cattle drover. He bought livestock in central Texas and moved the herds to Louisiana to market. Lee reenlisted in 1846 and served as a scout for Samuel Walker during the Mexican War. Mexicans were infiltrating America by the thousands and the Texas Rangers happened to encounter them; at that time they were outnumbered and beat a hasty retreat. The Texas Rangers served during the Mexican War between the United States and Mexico, 1846-48. Victory meant American acquisition of Arizona, California, Colorado, New Mexico, Nevada and Texas.

In 1848 to 1855, Lee was working with livestock. It was during this time that a man named Aikens made Lee a proposition of driving a large herd of horses to market into California. Lee and Aikens went to New Orleans to buy supplies. It was there that Lee espied a fine, silver pocket watch that would play a major role in his destiny. It had a good loud alarm and would come in handy. They rode to Brownsville, Texas where they hired a crew of 19 men.

The next project was to build up a herd. Lee accomplished that by buying and catching horses. At one point the crew embarked. Lee gathered horses as they traveled. They passed by many herds of wild horses; sometimes they captured a few of them. The horse herders moved through canyons, gulleys, prairies and valleys. At times they drove the herd along an arroyos or pathway along a dry stream bed.

The mustangers lived in the saddle and rode for hundreds of miles. Finally, they reached a beautiful valley with plenty of grass and running water for the herd. Lee decided to stay there for a few weeks to let the pregnant mares foal. Unknown to Lee was the danger that in the foothills of the mountains above them, Comanche spies were watching their every move.

In the camp, they began to unwind, wrestling and became rambunctious, horsing around as the cooks prepared supper. After dinner they sang songs and sat around the campfire telling stories. Lee took the first watch and rode Black Prince out to check the horse herd. All was calm, at midnight and he was relieved. He rolled his coat up for a pillow and pulled his horse blanket over him. A coyote howled, as Nelson crawled into the sack.

He had not slept long, when all hell broke loose. An Indian war cry, followed by another woke the entire camp. There were Comanche Indians everywhere. He sprang to his feet and went for his gun, when an Indian lasso circled his head. He was yanked off his feet. The warrior hogtied him. Except for Aikens, Lee, Martin and Stewart, the whole camp was massacred.

They were captured as slaves, stripped of their clothing and given deerskin shirts and leggings. A brave was going through Lee's things when he discovered the watch. The alarm went off at exactly three thirty, the time they usually rose. The Indian was astounded. Lee was tagged as a medicine man.

The Indians took everything: the horses, saddles, bridles, guns, ammo, tents, and bedding. They even stripped off the clothing, boots and any jewelry from the dead bodies. Pots, pans, utensils, canteens, all pillage were tied onto mules. The Comanche warriors finished by scalping the dead. The captives were taken down to view the dead.

At this point, the prisoners were mounted onto mules and tied hand and foot. At times they lost balance and started to fall over, to be caught and lifted back into position by the Indians. They started off and traveled most of the day and reached their camp in the early evening.

In front of the lodge were two logs with kindling in between. Two horses were shot and butchered. Strips of horse flesh were perforated by four foot saplings and held over the fire. Corn was ground in mortar and pestles into a mash.

The Comanche sat in a circle for their evening meal, which was served in dishes made of tree bark. The Indians ate holding the meat in the left hand and scooped the corn up in the right hand into the mouth. The braves took delight in flicking hot pieces of meat onto the skin of the captives in the center, which seared their flesh.

At the village all four men were bound and staked down to the ground. Lee did not sleep all night. At dawn, he was taken to the center of the village, the Comanche crowded together, trying to see the white man. The Indian with the watch gave it to the chief of the village. The

Chief handed the watch to his youngest wife, Moko, who gave Lee his pocket watch.

Lee held it up to the Sun-god and then listened to it, pretending it was telepathy from the gods. He set the watch, wound it and then waited, acting if he were a shaman with much magic. The alarm went off. The Indians stood in awe of him. They motioned for him to do it again, but he shook his head, no. He had been spared. The chief took Lee to be his personal slave. That night, Nelson slept in the chief's tent, though bound and staked down.

Lee awoke the next day and watched the chief of the Comanche Indian band. Big Wolf was middle aged and stood six feet tall. He had four younger wives. The youngest was most comely and he favored her. The chief had four children with them, who lived with their mothers, in separate cubicles, adjoined to his lodge. He summoned the wife he chose to sleep with.

Nelson Lee was now the slave of Chief Big Wolf of the Comanche band. He and the chief entered into a blood pact. Nelson basically signed an agreement to serve Big Wolf all of his life. Lee filled the chief's buffalo horn with water from the water shed, when he thirsted. He pounded corn in the mortar and pestle for his meals. Lee spread his buffalo skin for his rest and lit the chief's pipe for a smoke. He waited on Big Wolf hand and foot.

Lee was allowed the freedom to stroll within the village. He could sleep without fetters and could carry a knife. He had earned the chief's trust and was named "*Chemakacho,*" the good white man.

The Comanche male was a slovenly person, who slept a lot and did not work in camp. The women did all of the work. His only work was to hunt and go on the war trail. His scalps were his power and hung from his lodge. The fact that these Indians were unclean was true. They did not bathe regularly and tended to be smelly and dirty.

If the hunter shot a buffalo or killed a mustang for food, he rode into the village to inform his wife where it was. Her role was to ride out and find it, cut the flesh into strips and bring it to camp. If the husband shot a deer, he carried it across his saddle to his wife to dress and cook.

Lee was taken from the chief's teepee to the center of the village, where Aikens, Martin and Stewart were bound to stakes. Lee was bound in the same manner. Comanche warriors did a mock Scalp Dance around the captives, shaking knives and tomahawks in their faces. They circled around them giving out shrieks of war cries. They circled in a frenzied dance. The braves acted out scalping the men for a good two hours.

Then oddly enough, the men were freed. They were given Indian garb to wear and returned to camp. Aikens and Lee were able to talk in his tent. The Indians came and took Aikens from the tent and Lee surmised that Aiken was taken as a slave to another village, but he never saw him again. The next day Lee was given some menial chores.

That evening, Lee was again taken to the village center, where Martin and Stewart were bound to stakes in the ground and were naked. The Comanche warriors danced around them, giving out war-whoops. Like the night before, they circled them and shook knives and tomahawks in their faces. This went on for some time, as they mutilated them with their knives.

The eerie rhythmic tom-tom beat went on and on and then stopped. A sharp war cry followed. Martin and Stewart screamed in pain, as the devils took their scalps. They bled from their heads and all of the wounds. The blood pooled on the ground around them. The horrendous chanting and dancing continued, again. The frenzied Indians belted out war-cries and slashed the poor wretches.

Martin screamed in pain, "Oh Jesus, spare me from this agonizing pain." The drum beat reached a fevered pitch, and stopped. The Comanche raised their tomahawks and took their lives. He had lost his close comrades. Lee's life was spared, apparently because of the pocket watch.

A short time later, the Indian women of the village pulled down the teepees and rolled them up. The buffalo skins and clothing were packed travois. All of the work was done by the women. They loaded the mules and readied for the trip. After three days travel, they reached their destination, some 100 miles away. It was a small Comanche encampment, an extension of Big Wolf's tribe, called Manasaw. The Indian women hurried to put up the tents.

The Comanche raised some beans, corn and tobacco. Lee observed the celebration of the Green Corn Dance. Some 600 Indians attended the festival. Every family had a large pile of green corn beside a fire.

The Indians gathered in a huge circle. The celebration began and the Indians danced, and chanted, "ho, ho, ho, ho, ho." A crude drum, consisting of a wooden hoop with a buffalo skin stretched over it and tied in the back made the tom-tom instrument. It was played with a drumstick made from a buffalo bone.

Nelson Lee had been the slave of Chief Big Wolf, who sold his slave, Lee to another Comanche, Chief Spotted Leopard. Lee was later bartered away again, for a pile of animal skins, to a Chief Rolling Thunder.

Living in various villages, Lee had seen remnants of a Cavalry unit. On occasion he had caught sight of other white captives. When the women were stripped down to walk to the river for their daily baths, Lee saw fair skinned women, one with curly, red hair. In another village, he met some Mormon women slaves that spoke English and conversed with them.

Nelson described that the Comanche Indians wore war paint every day, including both sexes. War paint (body paint) came from clay, minerals and plants. The paint he wore was clay.

On one occasion, when traveling to another village, the Comanche happened onto a black bear. One horseman lassoed the bear's head, while another roped his back leg. Comanche horses backed up, stretching the bear, as one warrior cut its throat. They cooked the bear for supper.

Lee learned the Comanche language. He observed many festivals, the Comanche War Dance, Green Corn Dance, Pipe Dance, Roast-Dog-Dance and Scalp Dance. He observed Indian Wars and was treated like a Comanche for a three year period. He was a slave for chiefs and waited on them hand and foot to stay alive; his magic pocket watch helped save him.

Lee had waited the whole time of his capture for the right opportunity to escape. He tried on a couple of occasions to ease out of camp, but got caught. Finally, on a journey with Chief Rolling Thunder, Lee got his chance. The chief had grown quite thirsty on their trip. Discovering a running spring, the chief lay prostrate on the ground to get a drink.

Lee seized upon the opportunity and grabbed the chief's tomahawk and bludgeoned him in the head. He grabbed the chief's rifle, mounted his horse and retreated at a fast gallop. Lee traveled in the direction that they had just come. He rode hard to escape on the chief's horse with a mule tied behind. He followed an old animal trail. Nelson traveled over nearly impossible terrain and as the sun went down, he reached a small clearing surrounded by trees and slept.

Nelson knew that when the chief's body was found the Comanche would begin to search for him. He killed the mule and butchered it for food. Lee cut the meat into strips and built a small fire and roasted the meat. He ate hardily. He made a makeshift canteen from the bladder of the mule and hardened it over the fire and filled it with water, tying it off with a strand of buffalo skin.

Lee knew that animals had caught the scent of the dead mule. He learned to not sleep where he had killed an animal. Lee also did not forget the ways of the Comanche. He built up the fire and slept a troubled sleep. Nelson arose, having not slept much.

Lee traveled only about ten miles in the heavy brush and mountainous terrain, when nightfall was upon him. He had the mule meat and canteen, so he again slept. Nelson arose at the break of dawn, weary and sore. Lee rode until he came near a green valley. He had ridden about 30 miles. It was beautiful and calm, with a running stream. He watered his horse, bedded down and fell asleep around midnight.

Lee put as many miles between the dead Comanche chief and himself as he could. He rode for days and wandered in the mountains, before discovering a clear stream, with deer in the vicinity. Nelson fired his rifle for the first time, killing a plump doe. He kindled a fire and cooked the venison. He ate the steaks. Lee jerked the venison and rode on. After a week he looked down from a mountain and espied about 300 Indian lodges. He turned and retraced his route to escape before being caught.

On the twentieth day, Nelson again saw Indians. They were on the move, single file, probably going to visit another tribe. He watched until the last brave disappeared from view, before daring to cross the valley. Lee made good use of his rifle, killing enough deer to sustain him and found a clearing in the mountain pass with a spring at the base of a slope. A number of deer in the vicinity were feeding. Lee's horse was spent with broken hooves; his moccasins were worn out. He tied his hair back to keep it out of his face.

Nelson shot more deer and skinned them with his knife. He made a rough-shod deerskin shirt and leggings and a new pair of moccasins, hair inside for comfort. With plenty of venison, Lee mounted his horse and continued on.

He grew weaker by the day. Lee stopped, whenever he found water, but was very tired and suffered with pain. He prayed to God sometimes that when he fell asleep he would never wake up. Lee continued on, in agony.

On the 56th day of his departure, Lee came upon a rolling prairie. The horse grew more and more lame. At times he stopped to let him lie down and just rest. Finally, the horse could only be led. Lee removed the saddle and bridle and slapped the horse on the rump to set it free. Nelson took his buffalo skin and made a knapsack, tying it with the bridle reins. He picked up his rifle and canteen and hiked away, alone.

Lee became depressed and started to lose it. He doubted himself and had no horse. Lost and confused, he trudged along. He was sick at heart and bruised, in the middle of nowhere.

A few days of travel and Lee came upon a fountain pouring out of a rock. He refreshed himself and stayed the night. Lee awoke, close to a rolling prairie. He lay there a minute, when he heard a rifle crack. He decided Indians must be near.

Jumping to his feet, Lee awaited the consequences. To his amazement he heard singing and saw a Mexican Caballero with a wide brimmed hat, riding slowly with a deer across his saddle. He spoke to Lee in broken English. "How are you, senor?"

Not knowing his character, the Ranger spoke to him in Spanish and informed him that he was in dire straits and in need of help. The Comanchero asked him how he had come to be there. Lee explained that he had been lost in the mountains and was trying to reach civilization.

The Comanchero said that he had been on a trading expedition to the Apache Indians and was returning and that his companions were nearby. The Mexican went on to say that they were from San Fernandez, below Eagle Pass, near the Rio Grande.

The trader welcomed him to join them in camp. Concerned for Lee's well being, he dismounted and led the horse as Lee rode. The name of the good Samaritan was Joseph de Silva. The Comancheros were astonished to see the wild man, but welcomed him into their camp.

The Comancheros had eight pack mules laden with buffalo robes and furs from the Apache village. They rearranged the mule's loads to accommodate Lee riding one. He was treated with great kindness. The Mexican Traders had found Ranger Lee wandering in the wilderness; if it had not been for them happening along, he could have perished in the desert.

Lee accompanied Joseph de Silva and party all of the way to Matamoros, a seaport in northeastern Mexico, on the Rio Grande, where he sailed for New York. In New York, Nelson Lee wrote his memoirs, "Three Years Among the Comanches."

Cattle prices had been driven down during the Civil War when Texans were away fighting for the Confederacy. Cows were not taken to market and multiplied, driving the cost down. In 1866, they had depreciated to $4.00 a head. It became profitable to drive cattle to the stockyards in Abilene, Kansas. The size of cattle herds averaged around 2500 head. A crew was made up of a trail boss, horse handler, a cook, mess wagon, and a dozen drovers.

The Cherokee Indians trekked the long grueling journey from the eastern United States and arrived in Indian Territory in Oklahoma. They learned the way of the horse and hunted buffalo and began to raise cattle.

Jesse Chisolm was a rancher that was part Cherokee Indian. He was famous for beginning the Chisolm Trail from Texas north into Abilene to the slaughter-house in Kansas. The cattle were shipped east from there to Kansas City to the beef packers. In 1887, the Chisholm Trail reached a distance of 800 miles. They say that 6,000,000 beeves were herded up that long trail in those days, a place of cowboy legends.

#71. "Comanche Nation Flag"
Courtesy Footnote.com

Chapter Ten
Reservations

In 1843, Sam Houston, representing the Republic of Texas, sent Joseph C. Aldridge into the vicinity of Medicine creek to negotiate a treaty with the rebel Comanche Indians to keep them from raiding ranchers on the frontier. A treaty was reached, but Congress refused to draw a boundary line between Comancheria and the Republic of Texas.

In the 1850s, the U.S. government agreed upon assimilation and removal as the solution to acquiring Native American lands by the American government. Comanche and Kiowa Indians had resided in the vicinity of Fort Medicine Creek for some time. The Indian Appropriations Act of 1851 was an act that moved American Indian tribes onto reservations. Boundaries were established that surrounded the Indian reservations, which were protected by the U.S. government.

According to the government, reservations protected Native Americans from the growing population of whites moving westward. Actually the government removed the American Indians from the land so that white settlers could claim it. As the land was acquired from the Indians, more land was made available for the white settlers and the reservations became smaller and smaller. This act set the precedent for modern-day Native American reservations.

In 1865, Comanche Chief Ten Bears of the Yamparikas (Root-eaters) band signed the Treaty of the Little Arkansas River. As settlers came, the Comanche people were offered only a segment of their reservation to dwell on. In return, no white men would come there. That year, the pact was finalized and the reservation included much of western Oklahoma and Texas.

Comanche Indians that hunted off of the reservation were fined, while white men that went onto or hunted on reservation land were not. Comanche warriors, who were unhappy with the situation, attacked the trespassers.

In 1867, Chief Ten Bears spoke at the Medicine Lodge Treaty in Kansas and argued the Indian's side. The Comanche chief spoke and said, "I was born upon the prairie where the wind blew free, and there was nothing to break the light of the sun. I was born where there were no enclosures, and where everything drew free breath. I want to die there, and not within walls." - Ten Bears.

He said that the Army attacked first and the Comanche attacked second. He pleaded with the government to leave the Comanche people alone.

The Comanche Indians consented to a reservation, between the Red and Washita Rivers. The "Treaty of Medicine Bow Lodge," was signed in 1867 by the Apache, Arapaho, Cheyenne, Comanche, and Kiowa Indians. They were to be provided annuities, churches, and schools in return. The tribes were to allow the "Iron Horse," locomotives to cross their land, cease raiding and agree to live on the reservation. 60,000 square miles (38.5 million acres) were given up for the three million acre (4,800 square mile) reservation. These tribes were promised protection from the hunters, who were killing the buffalo only for their hides. The government broke their word and kept taking more land from the Comanche Indians. For all of Chief Ten Bear's efforts, the government reduced the size of the reservation again, solely in Oklahoma.

The Peace Treaty of 1867 was designed to bring calm to the Southern Plains, but Chief Quanah Parker of the Quahadi band refused to sign. The Comanche Indian majority surrendered at Fort Sill, Oklahoma, but Quanah was not among them. He and his band disappeared deeper into the plains and lived off the reservation for another seven years.

In 1868, a temporary post was established near Medicine Creek, known as Fort Medicine Bluff Creek, which became known as Camp Wichita; the camp was established along Medicine Creek on land inhabited by the Comanche, Kiowa and Wichita Indians.

Freed slaves that enlisted in the Army were assigned to black regiments of Cavalry and Infantry. Congress authorized that these regiments be transferred onto the Western Front to fight Indians. In June of 1868, Buffalo Soldiers were assigned to Camp Wichita on the Kiowa-Comanche reservation under General Philip Sheridan and Negro officer graduates from West Point took command of the black regiments.

In 1869, the 10th Infantry, with help from members of the Sixth Infantry, constructed a more permanent fort, known as Fort Sill. It was named by Major Philip H. Sheridan, after a classmate of his at West Point, General Joseph W. Sill, who was killed in action during the Civil War.

The government did not force the Comanche Indian people to remain on the reservation in 1869, nor did they enforce their staying there; the Peace-and–Reservation Policy was failing and the Comanche at home on the reservation was not working, either. Only, about two-thirds of the Comanche people arrived on the reservation, while the other one-third lived off and continued to hunt and make war as they had always done.

The Comanche people that chose the new reservation could not hunt or grow crops. The buffalo had been all but killed off by that time and the buffalo food source was gone. They had to depend solely on the government for food, shelter and clothing in order to survive.

Bands that remained off the reservation were constantly harassed and chased by U.S. Cavalry soldiers. Poor Comanche Indians were weak

Street parade of Comanche Indians. Lawton Okla

72. Comanches Ride in Parade
Lawton, Oklahoma, in 1905
Courtesy Western History Collections, University of Oklahoma Libraries

from hunger and suffering from the white man's disease. They welcomed reservation life over facing the bitter winter cold and famine.

On the reservation, Comanche people were urged to learn English and to farm, accept the white man's ways and religion; on the contrary, the Comanche kept their language and retained their heritage, culture and religion. They continued their powwows and passed down the stories.

The Indian children were expected to attend white schools. If the parents refused to send their children to school, the Indian agent withheld their food rations. Some Comanche children were sent to boarding schools in order to be changed, but they still retained their ways. On the reservation, they found that the government feared the Indian's power they received from their culture and religion and wanted them to give up their life style, fearing attack.

The first post commander at Fort Sill was Benjamin H. Grierson. The militia was dispatched from Fort Sill to fight in the Indian Wars on the Southern Plains after 1869 and the Red River War of 1874-75. The post served as a base for soldiers to scout the area and fight Indians on the warpath

Fort Sill became a place to conduct peace treaties. Soldiers were dispatched from there to protect Oklahoma settlers. In 1890 there were rumors of shutting the fort down. Instead, a number of field artillery regiments became stationed there, preserving the fort as the Secretary of War had dismissed the ideas of closing the fort, instead, it grew.

The new agent at Fort Sill, Oklahoma reservation for the Comanche, Kiowa and Kiowa-Comanche Indians was Mr. Laurie Tatum. He believed that the Indian's problems could be solved with gentleness and honesty and allowed no reservation Indians to be arrested or molested by the Army.

#73, "Comanche War-chiefs March in Parade"
Courtesy Western History Collections, University of Oklahoma Libraries

Tatum ordered the soldiers off of the reservation. The Indians still left the reservation and did not respond to his messages for them to return.

Indians camped near the reservation in teepees. The Comanche refused to farm or raise livestock. The only way they would work with cattle was to release a cow; the hunters would ride after the poor beast and shoot it with arrows and the women would go out and butcher it.

Congress offered various posts to religious segments. Episcopalians furnished an agent for the Sioux Indians and the Quakers provided an agent for the Comanche, Kiowa and Kiowa-Apache Indians. Agent Tatum's budget was cut to repay victims of the Comanche's raids. This left money short and lowered the food allowance; Indians had less to eat. They blamed the 1867 Treaty. The Comanche Indian were a proud people and disliked being expected to convert to the white man's life style. They wanted to be able to hunt the buffalo and retain their old way of life and did not want to become like white men.

The government removed the Indian's life source, the buffalo. Their lands to hunt were taken away. Comanche Indians depended more on government rations at the Fort Sill Indian reservation in order for them to live.

The agent told them that if the accepted the allotments that they would become citizens. The Comanche were lied to by the crooked agents. They had no desire to become U.S. Citizens, but remain the Comanche Shoshoni people, like they had been for thousands of years. Buffalo numbers were on the decline in the 19th Century, due to the government sponsored programs in 1871 for wholesale slaughter of the buffalo in order to force the Indians onto the reservations (1871-1879). Sixty five million buffalo were slaughtered because of this legislation devastating the Plains Indians. Beaver populations also, had declined sharply that had been trapped out for the fur trade. Horses were responsible, too for the decline

#74.
Apache Chief Geronimo
Courtesy Azusa Publishing
Company, LLC

#75. Geronimo's Militant Band
Courtesy Azusa Publishing Company, LLC

of the bison. Horses grazed on the same grasses as the buffalo and made buffalo hunting easier.

Ten Bears had served his tribe well. He was a peace chief and an honorable elder of the tribe. Ten Bears returned to the reservation at Fort Sill, Oklahoma and died in 1873.

In 1876, dissatisfied with reservation life, Chief Black Horse led a war party of 170 Comanche warriors off the reserve and headed for the Llano Estacado. On the war trail, Black Horse and his warrior band attacked the encampments of white buffalo hunters in Comancheria, which led to the Buffalo Hunter's War of 1877.

In the 1880's, Fort Sill served as a peace-time fort protecting settlers during the Oklahoma Land Run and the American Indians, like Chiricahua Apache Chief Geronimo, who was relocated there by the American government.

In 1887, Congress passed the General Allotment Act, which allowed reservations to be broken down into allotments. The allotments could be used by the Indians, however they were not pleased. The Comanche had always shared the land with their red brothers. Then, greedy white men tried to get them to divide and sell their land.

Pressures to allot and homestead the almost three-million-acre Kiowa, Comanche, and Apache Reservation intensified after passage of the 1889 Springer Amendment to the Indian Appropriation Bill that gave President Benjamin Harrison the authority to negotiate land sessions in western Indian Territory. Ceded reservation lands were incorporated into the newly formed Oklahoma Territory.

The former Michigan governor, David H. Jerome headed the "Jerome Commission," that negotiated the land sessions and gained notoriety after dealing with different tribes, so the K.C.A. peoples were wary when Jerome and his associates arrived at the Fort Sill agency on September 19, 1892.

The Jerome Agreement of 1892 was signed by the Kiowa, Comanche and Apache Indian tribes and the American government. The three tribes are commonly referred to as the K.C.A. The Jerome agreement allocated 160 acres of land to every man, woman and child (to be held in trust for them), but the Indian leaders asked $2.50 an acre and wound up with less. Instead, the act further reduced the size of the reserve to 480,000 acres at $1.25 per acre. The Indians forfeited their lands, with the exception of one half million acres (862 square miles) and agreed to accept two million dollars for relinquished lands. The Indians of the Southwestern Plains settled into a life of farming and ranching.

1897-1901, settlers encroached on Indian land, before it was open for white settlement. On June 5, 1901, the land allotments ended for the Indians and they began a life of farmers and ranchers. Indian children born after the allotments laws of 1901, were given land.

The Kiowa-Comanche-Apache and the Wichita-Caddo reservation opened on August 6, 1901. The reserve produced Kiowa, Caddo, and Comanche counties. County seats were in Hobart, Lawton and Anadarko.

The remainder of land was divided into tracts for a short time. In 1906, the government opened up the reservation land called "the Big Pasture," to white settlement, completing the allotment service, resulting in the termination of the "Homestead Act" in Oklahoma. It granted all children born after the Jerome Agreement was written, new allotments. After the turn of the century, Fort Sill housed the School of Fire in 1911, the Infantry School in 1913 and the first Aircraft School in 1915. During

World War II over 50,000 soldiers were trained there. In 1946, the U.S. Army Artillery Center was established there.

During World War II, a company of Comanche Indian Code-talkers served their country by speaking the Comanche tongue over the "walkie-talkies," the Japanese interpreters were confused by what they were saying and were not able to interpret the code. During W.W. II, The Wind Talkers used the Comanche language as code and helped save thousands of lives of soldiers. The Comanche soldiers were brave soldiers, considered heroes.

The Aviation School was moved to Fort Rucker, Alabama, where pilots in the Korean War were trained in aviation and warheads. An atomic artillery round was fired at Fort Sill in 1953 at Frenchman's Flat, Nevada. In the last half of the 20th century, Fort Sill gained popularity as one of the best Army bases in America and supported our interests in the Vietnam War. The fort helped build up the nearby city of Lawton, Oklahoma and surrounding towns, as-well-as helping to integrate business and schools.

In the 21st century, the Fort continued on as a U.S. Army Field Artillery Training Center for enlisted personnel, officers, U.S. Marine Corps and students from over 40 different countries, four brigades of Third Corps Artillery and nearly 15,000 soldiers. The Fort School of Aviation was moved to Fort Rucker, Alabama, where pilots in the Korean War were trained. Fort Sill supported America's interests during the Vietnam War.

Fort Sill manages the 146 square mile (93,828 acre Indian reserve). Fort Sill includes the Army Air field, Reynolds Army Community Hospital and the Fort Sill Museum and Army's largest collection of Military artifacts.

The Comanche tribe at present is 14,557 members strong. Nine miles north of Lawton, Oklahoma is the Comanche Nation complex. It employs one hundred forty five members of the tribe, who receive many services. Seven thousand, seven hundred sixty three members live on the Lawton-Fort Sill Reserve in Oklahoma, the rest reside in California, New Mexico and Texas.

The Comanche Nation headquarters is in Lawton, Oklahoma. The tribal area of jurisdiction extends to Caddo, Comanche, Cotton, Grady, Jefferson, Kiowa, Stephens and Tillman counties. Elections are held every three years. Michael Burgess is the present Tribal Chairman of the Comanche Nation. Vehicle tags are issued for the Comanche Nation. They own and operate ten tribal smoke shops and a bingo hall and four casinos: Comanche Nation Games, in Lawton, Comanche Red River Casino, in Devol, Comanche Spur Casino in Elgin, and Comanche Star Casino, in Walters.

The Comanche Tribe founded the Comanche Nation College (A two year college) in Lawton, Oklahoma. Annually every July, the Comanche Tribe hosts the Comanche Homecoming Powwow Celebration. In September, the Comanche Nation Fair is held in Walters, Oklahoma. Two dances a year are hosted by the Comanche Little Ponies over New Years and on May 22nd.

The Fort Bridger Great Treaty Council discussed the need for the Eastern Shoshoni Indians to have their own reservation. The Wind River Indian Reservation, established in central Wyoming by executive order.

The Eastern Shoshoni at the Wind River Reservation who were joined on the Wind River Reservation by the Northern Arapaho Indians. The Arapaho and Shoshoni Tribes operate two separate tribal governments. The reservation covers 2,268,008 acres housing 2650 Eastern Shoshonis. Income per capita is $4,340. Sixty per cent of the people have a high school degree and over 6% have a Bachelor's Degree.

Another reservation established for the Eastern Goshiute Shoshoni people was the reservation at Wind River. The famous Chief of the Green River and the Wind River Goshiute Shoshonis was Washakie. Chief Washakie was famous for taking six enemy scalps. The Goshiute Shoshonis spoke the Shoshonean language and their culture and tradition was Shoshoni Indian.

In 1863, the Goshiutes signed a treaty of peace and friendship at Tooele Valley. Chief Tabe was one of the signers. When the treaty of 1863 was written, Goshiute lands bounded on the north by the middle of the Great Desert, on the west by the Step-toe Valley and on the south by the Green Mountains and on the east by the Great Salt Lake, Tooele and Rush Valleys.

The Goshiute reservation was established on the Nevada-Utah border in 1914. The word Goshiute evolved from the word, Gutsipupuitsi, meaning "Desert People" or gutsip, in Shoshoni, meaning ashes, dry earth or dust.

Shoshoni reservations are the Wind River Reservation, in Wyoming, the Shoshoni-Bannock Reservation in Fort Hall, Idaho and the Duck Valley Shoshoni- Paiute Reservation, in Nevada. The Paiute-Shoshoni Indians dwell in the Bishop Colony in California. The Paiute-Shoshoni Tribe reside at the Fallon Reservation, in Nevada. The Paiute-Shoshoni Indians live at the Lone Pine Reservation in California. The Kiowa-Comanche-Apache Indian Reservation is at Fort Sill-Lawton, Oklahoma. The Caddo and Wichita Indian tribes dwell there, too.

INDEX

Bibliography

Bains, Rae, *Indians of the Plains*, Mahwah, New Jersey, Troll Associates, 1985.

Capps, Benjamin, *The Great Chiefs,* Time-Life, Alexandria, Virginia, 1975.

Convis, Charles L., *Warriors & Chiefs of the Old West*, Pioneer Press, Inc., Carson City, 1996.

Fehrenbach, T.R., *Comanches, The History of a People*, Anchor Books, New York, 1974.

Grant, Bruce, *Concise Encyclopedia of American Indians*, Random House, New York, 1989.

Gwynne, S.C., *Empire of the Summer Moon*, Scribner, New York, 2010.

Hagan, William T., *Quanah Parker, Comanche Chief,* University of Oklahoma Press, Norman, 1993.

Haines, Francis, *The Buffalo,* Thomas Y. Crowell Company, New York, 1970.

Haines, Francis, *Appaloosa, the Spotted Horse in Art and History*, Caballus Publishers, Lansing, 1963.

Inter-Tribal Council of Nevada, *Newe: A Western Shoshone History*, University of Utah Printing Service, Salt Lake, 1976.

Jahoda, Gloria, *The Trail of Tears*, Random House, New York, 1975.

Lee, Nelson, *Three Years Among the Comanches*, The Narrative Press, Santa Barbara, 2001.

Liljeblad, Sven, *The Idaho Indians in Transition*, 1805-1960, Idaho State University, Pocatello, Idaho, 1972.

Lund, Bill, *The Comanche Indians*, Bridgestone Books, Mankato, Minnesota, 1997.

Madsen, Brigham D., *The Northern Shoshoni*, Caxton Printers, Ltd., Caldwell, Idaho, 1980.

Mooney, Martin J., *The Comanche Indians*, Chelsea House Publishers, New York, 1993.

Neeley, Bill, *The Last Comanche Chief, The Life and Times of Quanah Parker,* Castle Books, New York, 2007

O'Neal, Bill, *Best of the West*, Lincolnwood, Illinois, Publications International, Ltd., 2006.

Utley, Robert M., *Encyclopedia of the American West,* Wings Books, New York, 1997.

Utley, Robert M., *Lone Star Justice,* Berkley Book Publishing Company, New York, 2002.

Wallace, Ernest & Hoebel, E. Adamson, *The Comanches, Lords of the Southern Plains,* University of Oklahoma Press, Norman, 1986.

Whistler, Clark, *Indians of the United States*, Doubleday, Garden City, New York, 1966.

Wyman, Walker D., *The Wild Horse of the West,* Caxton Printers, Ltd., Caldwell, Idaho, 1945.

Citing Electronic Publications

\<http://www.accessgeneology.com/native/tribes/kiowa/kiowaapache hist.htm\>

\<http://www.accessgeneology.com/native/tribe/wichita/wichita indianhist.htm\>

\<http://www.angelfire.com/realm/shades/nativeamericans/bison.htm\>

\<http://www.buffalosoldier.net\>

\<http://www.csp.org/communities/docs/fikes-nac_history.html\>

\<http://www.digital.library.okstate.edu/encyclopedia/entries/c/ch045.html\>

\<http://www.digital.library.okstate.edu/encyclopedia/entries/f/fo038.html\>

\<http://www.en.wikipedia.org/wiki/Battle_of_the_Alamo\>

\<http://www.footnote.com/page/1928_quanah_parker_the_comanche_nation/\>

\<http://www.infoplease.comce6/society/A0834977.html\>

\<http://www.lastoftheindependents.com/sandcreek.htm\>

\<http://www.legendsofamerica.com/na-commanche.html\>

\<http://www.loc.gov/rr/program/bib/ourdocs/Indian.html\>

\<http://www.lone-star.net/mall/texasinfo/mexicow.htm\>

\<http://www.lone-star.net/mall/texasinfo/shouston.htm\>

\<http://www.nationalcowboymuseum.org/research/ems/About/Gallery
    Guides/Weitzenhoffe\>

\<http://www.pbs.org/weta/thewest/people/a_c/austin.htm\>

\<http://www.pbs.org/wgbh/aia/part4/4p2959.html\>

\<http://www.snowowl.com/peoplecomanche.html\>

\<http://www.texasranger.org/history/RangersRepublic.htm\>

\<http://www.tshaonline.org/handbook/online/articles/btao1\>

\<http://www.tshaonline.org/handbook/online/articles/CC/dfc2.html\>

\<http://www.tshaonline.org/handbook/online/articles/qea01\>

The Author explores inside a 19th Century stone house in southeastern Oregon.

About the Author

Born in Lexington, Nebraska, Robert Bolen, B.A. has a degree in Archeology/ Anthropology. In Archeology class he was informed that because of his features, the Mongolian Eye-fold, that he was part Indian. In 1755 a Bolen ancestor was taken captive by Delaware Indians. She was later rescued with her baby daughter, Robb's Great, Great, Grandmother. At the time of rescue, the poor girl (just 17) was scalped, but lived. The French scalp was the size of a silver dollar. Family says that she combed her hair hiding the scar and managed to live to be over one hundred years of age. Bolen's served under George Washington in the American Revolution. In 1777 the author's ancestors erected Fort Bolin near Cross Creek, Pennsylvania for protection from Indian attacks. Two ancestors were killed in Kentucky by Shawnee Indians allied to the British. Great Granddad Gilbert Bolen rode with the Ohio Fourth Cavalry in the Civil War under General Sherman; in 1866, he brought his wife and six children west to Nebraska in a Conestoga wagon. Grand-dad Denver Colorado Bolen knew Buffalo Bill Cody in western Nebraska.

Bolen is an authority on Indian artifacts and trade beads. Robb and Dori Bolen reside in Nampa, near Boise, Idaho. Robb owns the website, Fort Boise Bead Trader.com.

PHOTOGRAPHS
COURTESY OF

AZUSA Publishing, LLC
3575 S. Fox Street
Englewood, CO 80110

Email: azusa@azusapublishing.com
Phone Toll-free: 888-783-0077
Phone/Fax: 303-783-0073

Mailing address:
AZUSA Publishing, LLC
P.O. Box 2526
Englewood, Co. 89150

CPSIA information can be obtained at www.ICGtesting.com
Printed in the USA
266613BV00002B/4/P